CREATIVE TOURISM

CREATIVE TOURISM

By

Thomas Walsh

DISCOVERY PUBLISHING HOUSE PVT. LTD.
NEW DELHI-110 002

Published by:
Tilak Wasan

DISCOVERY PUBLISHING HOUSE PVT. LTD.
4383/4B, Ansari Road, Darya Ganj
New Delhi-110 002 (India)
Phone : +91-11-23279245, 43596064-65
Fax : +91-11-23253475
E-mail : discoverypublishinghouse@gmail.com
namitwasan9@gmail.com
sales@discoverypublishinggroup.com
web : www.discoverypublishinggroup.com

***Reprinted:* 2018**

***First Edition:* 2011**

ISBN: 978-81-8356-897-5

Creative Tourism

Printed at:
Infinity Imaging Systems
Delhi

PREFACE

Creative tourism demand is related to the need for learning and experiencing the creative process - from textiles weaving in the Mapuche regions of Chile to icon-painting in Russia. In some outbound markets, like the USA, the demand is driven in strong traditions and proliferation of hobbies and craft making. And because the creative tourism doesn't need impressive historic buildings, UNESCO lists or famous events, its destinations extend to all kind of countries and cities - from Berlin and Barcelona to small villages along the Yantra river and the high planes of Peru. This geographical enlargement benefits communities that otherwise wouldn't have a shot in taking a piece of the profit in the cultural tourism.

The creative tourism is a form of cultural tourism - it counts on cultural assets to attract travelers to a destination. It is also a form of creative community's development - by stimulating the creative industries from outside, the local economy improves beyond the profits from tourism.

On the other side, the business model for creative tourism defers radically from the business model of conventional cultural tourism. First, it is based on a different resources. Cultural tourism is focused on iconic buildings, mega events (festivals, etc.), strong presence of historic heritage, vibrant cultural life at a destination and limited famous geographies.

Creative tourism has existed since tourism began, but has only recently been given its own name. Its originators are Greg Richards and Crispin Raymond, who have defined 'creative tourism' as "learning a skill on holiday that is part of the culture of the country or community being visited. Creative tourists develop their creative potential, and get closer to local people, through informal participation in interactive workshops and learning experiences that draw on the culture of their holiday destinations".

The concept of 'creative tourism' is continuing to develop. In 2006, the "Creative Cities Network" endorsed by UNESCO, agreed on the following working definition of creative tourism: "Creative Tourism is travel directed towards an engaged and authentic experience, with participative learning in the arts, heritage, or special character of a place. It provides a connection with those who reside in this place and create this living culture.

Tourism in Namibia has a history of being developed around state owned resorts in protected areas. The product has been predominantly of a self-catering nature, mainly for national and regional travellers. Today, tourism is becoming an increasingly vital component of livelihood strategies for the communal and private farmers. Traditional farming activities are being complemented with tourism at so called guest farms and communal area residents are organising themselves in conservancies to create benefits from wildlife tourism..

CONTENTS

CHAPTER 1

INTRODUCTION : AN OVERVIEW

Tourism that offers visitors a creative pursuit (including arts, crafts and cookery workshops), with the opportunity to stay in high quality accommodation, and to connect with local people in a distinctive destination.

"Tourism is too important to be left to the marketers. It needs to be managed and owned by the community to insure that the benefits are realized," Robert McNulty, the founder and president of Partners for Livable Communities, recently commented. When a destination's genuine culture and nature are preserved, visitors get a true sense of the place, which is what they are after. "People keep looking for originality. They don't want to recreate their experience in your town, they want to enjoy what the town has to offer." This concept is at the heart of the creative tourism experience.

Mr. McNulty will explore further the role of tourism, creativity, and community as one of the keynote speakers at the Santa Fe International Conference on Creative Tourism. The conference will be held at the new Santa Fe Community Convention Center, September 28-October 2, 2008 in Santa Fe, New Mexico.

The civic vision and ownership of tourism McNulty refers to also has long-lasting benefits for a city. "Tourism is a form of community development," McNulty continued. "Cities have needs that visitors can financially support. By balancing the tourism infrastructure with existing city services, the year-round resident has a higher quality of life." The goal of creative tourism is to engage visitors more completely by encouraging a deeper understanding of a place, increasing the vitality of the local tourism industry.

This community-based model is supported by Greg Richards - an originator of the 'creative tourism" concept, international authority on tourism, and another conference speaker. Said Julie Wilson in their 2007 book, Tourism, Creativity and Development, "...the concept of 'creative tourism' as originally conceived by Richards and Raymond places the onus on the destination to actively identify those areas of creativity, which can be anchored in the destination and developed as specific products and experiences." Using a creative tourism model, communities both preserve their heritage and make it available for visitors to experience.

While travelers are thinking hard about how to get the best vacation for their money in today's economic environment, creative tourism offers something with lasting value. The opportunities for visitors to interact with the local culture in an intimate way, deliver the kind of original experience Robert McNutly refers to, making return visits more likely and establishing tourists as an ongoing resource for the community.

The US tourism industry is expected to slow in 2008. However, over the next 10 years, the industry is predicted to grow, increasing the contribution to the US Gross Domestic Product from $5.899 billion in 2008 to $10.855 billion in 2018 and adding almost 580,000 jobs in the same time period, according to a study by the World Travel & Tourism Council. Through a comprehensive schedule of theoretical and practical activities, the Creative Tourism Conference intends to provide instruction on putting the creative tourism experience to work so communities can prosper during this future period of growth.

Mornings at the conference are planned for discussion. Afternoons will include useful sessions on creative tourism fundamentals, hands-on creative tourism experiences and how-to sessions for implementing creative tourism in a variety of ways, from agritourism to gastronomy to the arts. In addition to Mr. McNutly and Mr. Richards, the conference includes an outstanding group of guest lecturers and leaders in creativity and tourism from around the world who will help facilitate and guide conversation on various topics.

Finally, representatives of UNESCO's Creative Cities Network from Montreal, Edinburgh, Seville, Berlin, Bologna, Aswan, Popayan (Colombia), and Buenos Aries will be presenting ways in which their cities are using creative tourism. Santa Fe, with its rich cultural influences and highly-creative population, was designated the first UNESCO Creative City in the US and is a living example of creative tourism at work.

Recent research shows that people want more time, space and energy, and a greater sense of wellbeing. They are demonstrating a growing desire to connect with each other and feel more in touch with local communities. Some of this can be achieved through creative tourism as it provides visitors with the opportunity to learn a new skill, provide a sense of achievement and to create a unique souvenir, for example, a painting, crafted object or food product. This type of break is also more likely to give people a lasting emotional attachment to the destination and will encourage them to recommend and also revisit the destination.

Every now and then, it's great to get away from daily routine and familiar surroundings to gain some new perspectives. A recent trip to France gave some insights into what generates the tourism economy. It's not that difficult to figure out what tourists want: Just look at what they line up for.

Take museums in Paris. Apparently there's a shortage of good art in the world, which for many cynics of contemporary art is no surprise. I was warned that lineups at the Louvre are nasty, but that they are much shorter at the Musée d'Orsay just across the river. It's Paris's best-kept secret.

The secret is out. The morning we arrived at the Musée d'Orsay, there was a crowd of more than 500 standing outside on the plaza, waiting to get in the door. The 12-euro entrance fee was not high enough to deter these desperate art patrons. They were willing to wait a couple of hours in line on top of the admission fee.

Tourists stand in line for more than just art. They'll stand in line to buy stuff, too. Galeries Lafayette, the famous department store in Paris, makes our high-end retailers look like convenience stores. The queues weren't quite as long as those at the Musée d'Orsay, but they did add to the total "cost" of buying a Hermès scarf or Dior bag.

The queue to go up the Eiffel Tower was a nightmare of its own; we took our pictures from the bottom looking up.

Lineups indicate what global tourists want to see and do - and they will pay big bucks to do it. Culture, shopping, entertainment, experiences: There is a huge global demand for these things. Haven't the crazed mobs at the Louis Vuitton flagship store on the Champs Élysées heard that the global economy is on the skids? High-end tourism seems to be recession proof.

Tourism marketing specialists in Canada are well aware of the dilemma. How can we become an international destination when we don't have the museums, the history, the sidewalk cafés, or the miles of shopping that make up Paris? There must be a strategy to tap into the gold mine of all those tourists standing in line in Paris.

Play to our strengths? Sounds reasonable enough, but Canada has more fly-fishing, whale-watching and pristine forests than there appears to be global demand. I've never seen 500 people line up to rent camping gear (although the parking lots in Banff and Niagara Falls can be daunting). Our beautiful surroundings are certainly an asset, but let's be honest: The tourism market for these experiences are limited.

The onus is on Canada to find its own niche in the tourism world. We need to build some merchandising brand names in our own country that will make it a destination on its own. Why would an international visitor go shopping in Yorkville when all the merchandise is French, Italian or American? Why not just go to Paris, Milan or Los Angeles?

We need to attract and foster a growing concentration of Canadian artists, designers and creators. In a Paris bookstore, I noticed a display of gorgeous books on architecture. It was a series of books highlighting contemporary building design in several countries: France, the U.S., Holland, Brazil, Sweden, Spain, Italy, Australia and even Mexico. (Mexico!) Where was Canada's book? There wasn't one, and that's a shame. It perpetuates the myth we are all log cabins and igloos.

It is only a matter of concentrated effort to turn Canada into a "must-see" destination for the global tourist. Another thing I learned on vacation was that all the international people we met along the way - French, Danes, Brits, New Zealanders - certainly seem to like Canada well enough. All they need now is a reason to visit.

Even with the current downturn in the economy many people still feel that a holiday is fundamental and a destination that offers the opportunity to learn something at the same time as providing a change of scene will gain a competitive edge.

Carnival Cruises has released details of the attractions that will feature on board its latest cruise liner, the Carnival Magic, when it debuts next May.

The 3,690-passenger vessel is the newest "fun ship" from Carnival, which says that it will contain several firsts for both the cruise line and the industry.

An on-board pub, complete with home-brew beer is one of the concepts, along with the first ropes course at sea, a net course suspended above deck that offers guests (with the stomach for it) views of the sea 150 feet (45m) below.

Another attraction is the on-board WaterWorks aqua park, which features a "Twister" spiral slide and a splash park complete with 500-gallon (1,890 liter) "dump bucket" which is aimed at youngsters and families.

Echoing the open-air promenade features found on the Oasis of the Seas, which debuted last year from Royal Caribbean, Carnival Magic will also feature a half mile (0.8 km) promenade which encircles a deck so that guests can stretch their legs.

The 130,000-ton ship is set to be one of the largest to launch next year, despite holding fewer passengers than the 128,000-ton Disney Dream, which is set to make its maiden voyage in January.

Disney Dream features the four-storey high-speed log ride "Aquaduck," which sounds pretty fun itself, extending 16 feet (nearly 5 meters) off the edge of the ship at one point, before a sharp turn back to safety.

She will also offer fun-loving guests "Goofy's Sports Deck", "Nemo's Reef" and the "Donald Pool."

If you are interested in developing workshops for the visitor market we would also love to hear from you and am particularly interested in;

- Visual artists for watercolour, pastel and oil painting
- Sculptors
- Potters
- Metalworkers
- Jewellers
- Furniture makers
- Glassmakers
- Wood carvers
- Craftspeople for knitting, textiles, weaving, embroidery
- Traditional Kentish crafts e.g. beer making, decorating with hops
- Chefs cooking with local Kent produce, e.g. oysters, mussels, fish, food foraged in the Kent countryside
- Food producers for cheese making, cooking with apples etc.
- Vineyards for winemaking, farms/orchards for cider, apple juice

There is a significant market of people looking for deeper and more satisfying experiences where they can actually participate and also connect with local people and feel part of the community they are visiting. Other countries and areas around the world are developing this type of tourism product and I have been particularly inspired by the ideas of Greg Richards and Crispin Raymond and the creative tourism work they have undertaken in New Zealand.

Tourism is travel for recreational, leisure or business purposes. The World Tourism Organization defines tourists as people who "travel to and stay in places outside their usual environment for more than twenty-four (24) hours and not more than one consecutive year for leisure, business and other purposes not related to the exercise of an activity remunerated from within the place visited." Tourism has become a popular global leisure activity. In 2008, there were over 922 million international tourist arrivals, with a growth of 1.9% as compared to 2007. International tourism receipts grew to US$944 billion (euro 642 billion) in 2008, corresponding to an increase in real terms of 1.8%.

Tourism is vital for many countries, such as Egypt, Greece, Lebanon, Spain and Thailand, and many island nations, such as The Bahamas, Fiji, Maldives, and the Seychelles, due to the large intake of money for businesses with their goods and services and the opportunity for employment in the service industries associated with tourism. These service industries include transportation services, such as airlines, cruise ships and taxicabs, hospitality services, such as accommodations, including hotels and resorts, and entertainment venues, such as amusement parks, casinos, shopping malls, music venues and theatres.

Theobald (1994) suggested that "etymologically, the word tour is derived from the Latin, 'tornare' and the Greek, 'tornos', meaning 'a lathe or circle; the movement around a central point or axis'. This meaning changed in modern English to represent 'one's turn'. The suffix -ism is defined as 'an action or process; typical behavior or quality', while the suffix, -ist denotes 'one that performs a given action'. When the word tour and the suffixes -ism and -ist are combined, they suggest the action of movement around a circle. One can argue that a circle represents a starting point, which ultimately returns back to its beginning. Therefore, like a circle, a tour represents a journey in that it is a round-trip, i.e., the act of leaving and then returning to the original starting point, and therefore, one who takes such a journey can be called a tourist."

In 1941, Hunziker and Krapf defined tourism as people who travel "the sum of the phenomena and relationships arising from the travel and stay of non-residents, insofar as they do not lead to permanent residence and are not connected with any earning activity." In 1976, the Tourism Society of England's definition was: "Tourism is the temporary, short-term movement of people to destination outside the places where they normally live and work and their activities during the stay at each destination. It includes movements for all purposes." In 1981, the International Association of Scientific Experts in Tourism defined tourism in terms of particular activities selected by choice and undertaken outside the home.

TOURISTS: CHOOSING HOLIDAY DESTINATION

Tourists rate safety as their number one concern when choosing their holiday destination according to new data released today by the FIA on World Tourism Day.

Lack of safety whether due to crime, the risk of natural disasters, sanitary risks or terrorism, was the principle reason to rule out a destination, and scored highest in the survey with 8.5 points out of a possible 10. Safety was closely followed by weather which received an average 8.2 points, quality of accommodation received 8.2 points, and natural beauty 8.0 points.

The data, based on a survey conducted by the FIA, highlighted the need for tourism organisations and governments to ensure that tourists are provided with adequate information on the areas with a higher risk, maximise security measures, and establish common information and evacuation protocols for all countries in cases of disaster or health risks.

The factors that were the least valued by tourists in choosing a destination included the availability of sports facilities (4.8) and nightlife (4.9), although the latter was the highest valued factor among travellers aged 18 to 30 years. Likewise, availability of sports facilities was more important for tourists aged 18 to 45 than those aged 46 and older.

Presence of natural beauty in the surrounding area, including quality of beaches and other swimming areas, scored significantly higher in importance than quality of food or other tourist attractions.

The survey also revealed that most tourists travelled to countries within their own continent. For example Southern Europe was noted as the most frequent destination region of European travellers. However, younger respondents from 18 to 30 years old travelled to a greater degree to destinations outside of Europe compared with older respondents.

In 1994, the United Nations classified three forms of tourism in its Recommendations on Tourism Statistics:

- Domestic tourism, involving residents of the given country traveling only within this country.
- Inbound tourism, involving non-residents traveling in the given country.
- Outbound tourism, involving residents traveling in another country.

WORLD TOURISM STATISTICS AND RANKINGS

Most Visited Countries by International Tourist Arrivals

In 2008, there were over 922 million international tourist arrivals, with a growth of 1.9% as compared to 2007. In 2009, international tourists arrivals fell to 880 million, representing a worldwide decline of 4% as compared to 2008. The region most affected was Europe with a 6% decline.

The World Tourism Organization reports the following ten countries as the most visited from 2006 to 2009 by the number of international travelers. When compared to 2006, Ukraine entered the top ten list, surpassing Russia, Austria and Mexico, and in 2008, surpassed Germany. In 2008, the U.S. displaced Spain from the second place. Most of the top visited countries continue to be on the European continent.

In 2009, Malaysia made it into the top 10 most visited countries' list. Malaysia secured the ninth position, just below Turkey and Germany. In 2008, Malaysia was in 11th position. Both Turkey and Germany climbed one rank in arrivals, occupying seventh and eighth positions respectively, while France continued to lead the ranks in terms of tourist arrivals.

Rank	Country	UNWTO Regional Market	International tourist arrivals (2009)	International tourist arrivals (2008)	International tourist arrivals (2007)	International tourist arrivals (2006)
1	France	Europe	74.2 million	79.2 million	80.9 million	77.9 million
2	U.S.	North America	54.9 million	57.9 million	56.0 million	51.0 million
3	Spain	Europe	52.2 million	57.2 million	58.7 million	58.0 million
4	China	Asia	50.9 million	53.0 million	54.7 million	49.9 million
5	Italy	Europe	43.2 million	42.7 million	43.7 million	41.1 million
6	U.K.	Europe	28.0 million	30.1 million	30.9 million	30.7 million
7	Turkey	Europe	25.5 million	25.0 million	22.2 million	18.9 million
8	Germany	Europe	24.2 million	24.9 million	24.4 million	23.6 million
9	Malaysia	Asia	23.6 million	22.1 million	21.0 million	17.5 million
10	Mexico	North America	21.5 million	22.6 million	21.4 million	21.4 million

INTERNATIONAL TOURISM RECEIPTS

International tourism receipts grew to US$944 billion (€642 billion) in 2008, corresponding to an increase in real terms of 1.8% from 2007. When the export value of international passenger transport receipts is accounted for, total receipts in 2008 reached a record of US$1.1 trillion, or over US$3 billion a day.

The World Tourism Organization reports the following countries as the top ten tourism earners for the year 2009. It is noticeable that most of them are on the European continent, but the United States continues to be the top earner.

Rank	Country	UNWTO Regional Market	International tourist arrivals (2009)	International tourist arrivals (2008)	International tourist arrivals (2007)	International tourist arrivals (2006)
1	United States	North America	$94.2 billion	$110.1 billion	$97.1 billion	$85.8 billion
2	Spain	Europe	$53.2 billion	$61.6 billion	$57.6 billion	$51.1 billion
3	France	Europe	$48.7 billion	$55.6 billion	$54.3 billion	$46.3 billion
4	Italy	Europe	$40.2 billion	$45.7 billion	$42.7 billion	$38.1 billion
5	China	Asia	$39.7 billion	$40.8 billion	$37.2 billion	$33.9 billion
6	Germany	Europe	$34.7 billion	$40.0 billion	$36.0 billion	$32.8 billion
7	U.K.	Europe	$30.1 billion	$36.0 billion	$38.6 billion	$34.6 billion
8	Australia	Oceania	$25.6 billion	$24.8 billion	$22.3 billion	$17.8 billion
9	Turkey	Europe	$21.3 billion	$22.0 billion	$18.5 billion	$16.9 billion
10	Austria	Europe	--	$21.8 billion	$18.9 billion	$16.6 billion

International Tourism Expenditures

The World Tourism Organization reports the following countries as the top ten biggest spenders on international tourism for the year 2009. For the fifth year in a row, German tourists continue as the top spenders.

Rank	Country	UNWTO Regional Market	International tourist arrivals (2009)	International tourist arrivals (2008)	International tourist arrivals (2007)	International tourist arrivals (2006)
1	Germany	Europe	$80.8 billion	$91.0 billion	$83.1 billion	$73.9 billion
2	U.S.	North America	$73.1 billion	$79.7 billion	$76.4 billion	$72.1 billion
3	U.K.	Europe	$48.5 billion	$68.5 billion	$71.4 billion	$63.1 billion
4	China	Asia	$43.7 billion	$36.2 billion	$29.8 billion	$24.3 billion
5	France	Europe	$38.9 billion	$43.1 billion	$36.7 billion	$31.2 billion
6	Italy	Europe	$27.8 billion	$30.8 billion	$27.3 billion	$23.1 billion
7	Japan	Asia	$25.1 billion	$27.9 billion	$26.5 billion	$26.9 billion
8	Canada	North America	$24.3 billion	$26.9 billion	$24.7 billion	$20.6 billion
9	Russia	Europe	$20.8 billion	$23.8 billion	$21.2 billion	$18.1 billion
10	Netherlands	Europe	$20.7 billion	$21.7 billion	$19.1 billion	$17.0 billion

Most Visited Cities

Top 10 most visited cities by estimated number of international visitors by selected year

City	Country	International visitors (millions)	Year/Notes
Paris	France	14.8	2009 (Excluding extra-muros visitors)
London	United Kingdom	14.1	2009
Bangkok	Thailand	10.21	2008 (External study estimation)
Singapore	Singapore	9.7	2009
Kuala Lumpur	Malaysia	8.94	2008 (External study estimation)
Hong Kong	China	8.9	2009
New York City	United States	8.7	2009
Dubai	United Arab Emirates	7.58	2008
Istanbul	Turkey	7.51	2009
Shanghai	China	6.7	2007

Travelling Abroad

Wealthy people have always travelled to distant parts of the world, to see great buildings, works of art, learn new languages, experience new cultures and to taste different cuisines. Long ago, at the time of the Roman Republic, places such as Baiae were popular coastal resorts for the rich. The word tourism was used by 1811 and tourist by 1840. In 1936, the League of Nations defined foreign tourist as "someone traveling abroad for at least twenty-four hours". Its successor, the United Nations, amended this definition in 1945, by including a maximum stay of six months.

Leisure Travel

Leisure travel was associated with the Industrial Revolution in the United Kingdom - the first European country to promote leisure time to the increasing industrial population. Initially, this applied to the owners of the machinery of production, the economic oligarchy, the factory owners and the traders. These comprised the new middle class. Cox & Kings was the first official travel company to be formed in 1758.

The British origin of this new industry is reflected in many place names. In Nice, France, one of the first and best-established holiday resorts on the French Riviera, the long esplanade along the seafront is known to this day as the Promenade des Anglais; in many other historic resorts in continental Europe, old, well-established palace hotels have names like the Hotel Bristol, the Hotel Carlton or the Hotel Majestic - reflecting the dominance of English customers.

Many leisure-oriented tourists travel to the tropics, both in the summer and winter. Places of such nature often visited are: Mexico, Bali in Indonesia, Brazil, Cuba, the Dominican Republic, Malaysia, the various Polynesian tropical islands, Queensland in Australia, Thailand, and Florida and Hawaii in the United States.

Winter Tourism

Major ski resorts are located in the various European countries (e.g. Austria, Bulgaria, Czech Republic, France, Germany, Iceland, Italy, Norway, Poland, Sweden, Slovenia, Spain, Switzerland), Canada, the United States, New Zealand, Japan, South Korea, Chile and Argentina.

Improvements in Technology

Mass tourism could only have developed with the improvements in technology, allowing the transport of large numbers of people in a short space of time to places of leisure interest, so that greater numbers of people could begin to enjoy the benefits of leisure time.

In the United States, the first seaside resorts in the European style were at Atlantic City, New Jersey and Long Island, New York.

In Continental Europe, early resorts included: Ostend, popularized by the people of Brussels; Boulogne-sur-Mer (Pas-de-Calais) and Deauville (Calvados) for the Parisians; and Heiligendamm, founded in 1793, as the first seaside resort on the Baltic Sea.

Adjectival tourism refers to the numerous niche or specialty travel forms of tourism that have emerged over the years, each with its own adjective. Many of these have come into common use by the tourism industry and academics. Others are emerging concepts that may or may not gain popular usage. Examples of the more common niche tourism markets include:

- Agritourism
- Culinary tourism
- Cultural tourism
- Ecotourism
- Extreme tourism
- Geotourism
- Heritage tourism
- LGBT tourism
- Medical tourism
- Nautical tourism
- Pop-culture tourism
- Poverty tourism
- Religious tourism
- Space tourism
- War tourism
- Wildlife tourism

Recent Developments

There has been an upmarket trend in the tourism over the last few decades, especially in Europe, where international travel for short breaks is common. Tourists have high levels of disposable income, considerable leisure time, are well educated, and have sophisticated tastes. There is now a demand for a better quality products, which has resulted in a fragmenting of the mass market for beach vacations; people want more specialised versions, quieter resorts, family-oriented holidays or niche market-targeted destination hotels.

The Travel and Tourism Competitiveness Report was first published in 2007 by the World Economic Forum. The 2007 report covered 124 major and emerging economies. The 2008 report covered 130 countries, and the 2009 report expanded to 133 countries. The index is a measurement of the factors that make it attractive to develop business in the travel and tourism industry of individual countries, rather than a measure of a country attractiveness as a tourist destination. The report ranks selected nations according to the Travel and Tourism Competitiveness Index (TTCI), which scores from 1 to 6 the performance of a given country in each specific subindex. The overall index is made of three main subindexes: (1) regulatory framework; (2) business environment and infrastructure; and (3) human, cultural, and natural resources. The Report also includes a specific Country Profile for each of the nations evaluated, with each of the scores received to estimate its TTCI, and complementary information regarding key economic indicators from the World Bank, and country indicators from the World Travel and Tourism Council.

For the 2008 index, each of the three main subindexes is made of the scoring of the following 14 variables, called pillars in the TTC Report. Several changes were introduced in the 2008 TTCI in the definition of the variables as compared to the definitions of the 2007 TTCI. First, the "environmental regulation" pillar was improved with help from the IUCN and the UNWTO, and for the 2008 index was re-named the "environmental sustainability" pillar to "better reflect its components and to capture the increasingly recognized importance of sustainability in the sector's development." Second, the original pillar "natural and cultural resources" was divided into two separate subcomponents: "natural resources" and "cultural resources", thus, allowing to differentiate those countries which do not necessarily have the same strengths or weaknesses in these two different resources. In general, the model was improved with better data and new concepts were introduced. The 2009 report kept the same 14 variables.

Pillars by Subindexes

Regulatory framework	Business environment and infrastructure	Human, cultural, and natural resources
Policy rules and regulations	Air transport infrastructure	Human resources
Environmental sustainability	Ground transport infrastructure	Affinity for Travel & Tourism
Safety and security	Tourism infrastructure	Natural resources
Health and hygiene	Information and Communications Techn. infrastr.	Cultural resources
Prioritization of Travel and Tourism	Price competitiveness in T&T industry	

The developments in technology and transport infrastructure, such as jumbo jets, low-cost airlines and more accessible airports have made many types of tourism more affordable. WHO estimates that up to 500,000 people are on planes at any time. There have also been changes in lifestyle, such as retiree-age people who sustain year round tourism. This is facilitated by internet sales of tourism products. Some sites have now started to offer dynamic packaging, in which an inclusive price is quoted for a tailor-made package requested by the customer upon impulse.

There have been a few setbacks in tourism, such as the September 11 attacks and terrorist threats to tourist destinations, such as in Bali and several European cities. Also, on December 26, 2004, a tsunami, caused by the 2004 Indian Ocean earthquake, hit the Asian countries on the Indian Ocean, including the Maldives. Thousands of lives were lost and many tourists died. This, together with the vast clean-up operation in place, has stopped or severely hampered tourism to the area.

The terms tourism and travel are sometimes used interchangeably. In this context, travel has a similar definition to tourism, but implies a more purposeful journey. The terms tourism and tourist are sometimes used pejoratively, to imply a shallow interest in the cultures or locations visited by tourists.

Sustainable Tourism

"Sustainable tourism is envisaged as leading to management of all resources in such a way that economic, social and aesthetic needs can be fulfilled while maintaining cultural integrity, essential ecological processes, biological diversity and life support systems." (World Tourism Organization)

Sustainable development implies "meeting the needs of the present without compromising the ability of future generations to meet their own needs" (World Commission on Environment and Development, 1987)

ECOTOURISM

Ecotourism, also known as ecological tourism, is responsible travel to fragile, pristine, and usually protected areas that strives to be low impact and (often) small scale. It helps educate the traveler; provides funds for conservation; directly benefits the economic development and political empowerment of local communities; and fosters respect for different cultures and for human rights.

Pro-poor Tourism

The potential tourism has to help the very poorest in developing countries has been receiving increasing attention by those involved in development and the issue has been addressed either through small scale projects in local communities and by Ministries of Tourism attempting to attract huge numbers of tourists. Research by the Overseas Development Institute suggests that neither is the best way to encourage tourists' money to reach the poorest as only 25% or less (far less in some cases) ever reaches the poor; successful examples of money reaching the poor include mountain climbing in Tanzania or cultural tourism in Luang Prabang, Laos. For tourism to successfully reach the poor efforts must be made for tourists to use local currency, for locals to develop relevant skills and to ensure that exclusive contracts do not dominate the sector.

Recession Tourism

Recession tourism is a travel trend, which evolved by way of the world economic crisis. Identified by American entrepreneur Matt Landau (2007), recession tourism is defined by low-cost, high-value experiences taking place of once-popular generic retreats. Various recession tourism hotspots have seen business boom during the recession thanks to comparatively low costs of living and a slow world job market suggesting travelers are elongating trips where their money travels further.

MEDICAL TOURISM

When there is a significant price difference between countries for a given medical procedure, particularly in Southeast Asia, India, Eastern Europe and where there are different regulatory regimes, in relation to particular medical procedures (e.g. dentistry), traveling to take advantage of the price or regulatory differences is often referred to as "medical tourism".

Educational Tourism

Educational tourism developed, because of the growing popularity of teaching and learning of knowledge and the enhancing of technical competency outside of the classroom environment. In educational tourism, the main focus of the tour or leisure activity includes visiting another country to learn about the culture, such as in Student Exchange Programs and Study Tours, or to work and apply skills learned inside the classroom in a different environment, such as in the International Practicum Training Program.

The Historical Archive on Tourism (HAT, Historisches Archiv zum Tourismus) is sited in the city of Berlin at the Freie Universität Berlin, housed at the Willy-Scharnow-Institut für Tourismus. The HAT had been founded in 1989; today the length of the shelves amounts to some 500 running meter. The focus of the material is not on "travel" generally but on "tourism" as a special sort of travelling. The HAT is probably the biggest archive in this field, gathering various materials ranging from Baedekers to private photo albums, in particular there is an extensive collection of flyers and other so-called ephemera. Mainly the material stems from Central Europe, in particular from Germany, but nearly all other parts of the world are also represented, e.g. Southern Africa or USA. Over 50,000 leaflets are stored, and some 200 journals and 10,000 books are registered. In addition statistics, posters and maps are gathered. The bulk of the material is from the 19th and 20th century, some books date back to around 1600. No OPAC is installed but short lists are published in the Internet.

Creative Tourism

Creative tourism has existed as a form of cultural tourism, since the early beginnings of tourism itself. Its European roots date back to the time of the Grand Tour, which saw the sons of aristocratic families traveling for the purpose of mostly interactive, educational experiences. More recently, creative tourism has been given its own name by Crispin Raymond and Greg Richards, who as members of the Association for Tourism and Leisure Education (ATLAS), have directed a number of projects for the European

Commission, including cultural and crafts tourism, known as sustainable tourism. They have defined "creative tourism" as tourism related to the active participation of travellers in the culture of the host community, through interactive workshops and informal learning experiences.

Meanwhile, the concept of creative tourism has been picked up by high-profile organizations such as UNESCO, who through the Creative Cities Network, have endorsed creative tourism as an engaged, authentic experience that promotes an active understanding of the specific cultural features of a place.

More recently, creative tourism has gained popularity as a form of cultural tourism, drawing on active participation by travelers in the culture of the host communities they visit. Several countries offer examples of this type of tourism development, including the United Kingdom, the Bahamas, Jamaica, Spain, Italy and New Zealand.

Visit to Dark Sites

One emerging area of special interest tourism has been identified by Lennon and Foley (2000) as "dark" tourism. This type of tourism involves visits to "dark" sites, such as battlegrounds, scenes of horrific crimes or acts of genocide, for example: concentration camps. Dark tourism remains a small niche market, driven by varied motivations, such as mourning, remembrance, education, macabre curiosity or even entertainment. Its early origins are rooted in fairgrounds and medieval fairs.

Advent of E-commerce

The World Tourism Organization (UNWTO) forecasts that international tourism will continue growing at the average annual rate of 4 %. With the advent of e-commerce, tourism products have become one of the most traded items on the internet. Tourism products and services have been made available through intermediaries, although tourism providers (hotels, airlines, etc.) can sell their services directly. This has put pressure on intermediaries from both on-line and traditional shops.

It has been suggested there is a strong correlation between tourism expenditure per capita and the degree to which countries play in the global context. Not only as a result of the important economic contribution of the tourism industry, but also as an indicator of the degree of confidence with which global citizens leverage the resources of the globe for the benefit of their local economies. This is why any projections of growth in tourism may serve as an indication of the relative influence that each country will exercise in the future.

Space tourism is expected to "take off" in the first quarter of the 21st century, although compared with traditional destinations the number of tourists in orbit will remain low until technologies such as a space elevator make space travel cheap.

Technological improvement is likely to make possible air-ship hotels, based either on solar-powered airplanes or large dirigibles. Underwater hotels, such as Hydropolis, expected to open in Dubai in 2009, will be built. On the ocean, tourists will be welcomed by ever larger cruise ships and perhaps floating cities.

Sports travel

Since the late 1970s packaged sports travel has become increasingly popular. Events such as rugby and football World Cups have enabled specialist travel companies to gain official ticket allocation and then sell them in packages that include flights, hotels and excursions.

Latest Trends

As a result of the late-2000s recession, international arrivals suffered a strong slowdown beginning in June 2008. Growth from 2007 to 2008 was only 3.7% during the first eight months of 2008. The Asian and Pacific markets were affected and Europe stagnated during the boreal summer months, while the Americas performed better, reducing their expansion rate but keeping a 6% growth from January to August 2008. Only the Middle East continued its rapid growth during the same period, reaching a 17% growth as compared to the same period in 2007. This slowdown on international tourism demand was also reflected in the air transport industry, with a negative growth in September 2008 and a 3.3% growth in passenger traffic through September. The hotel industry also reports a slowdown, as room occupancy continues to decline. As the global economic situation deteriorated dramatically during September and October as a result of the global financial crisis, growth of international tourism is expected to slow even further for the remaining of 2008, and this slowdown in demand growth is forecasted to continue into 2009 as recession has already hit most of the top spender countries, with long-haul travel expected to be the most affected by the economic crisis. This negative trend intensified as international tourist arrivals fell by 8% during the first four months of 2009, and the decline was exacerbated in some regions due to the outbreak of the influenza AH1N1 virus.

According to the latest statistics released by MasterCard on July 2, Shanghai Expo has already become a main target of foreign tourists' visiting Shanghai.

The survey says among those foreign tourists who plan to travel in Shanghai, nearly half of them would like to visit Expo Site and experience the Shanghai World Expo, including 80 percent of Hong Kongers, 48 percent of Japanese and 46 percent of Taiwanese.

Human Right

On the 15th of April 2010, European Commissioner Antonio Tajani attracted attention and criticism after the British newspaper, The Sunday Times, reported he had unveiled a plan declaring tourism as a human right. According to the article, pensioners, youths and those too poor to afford it should have their travel subsidised by the taxpayer. Tajani's program will be piloted until 2013 and then put into full operation. In introducing his plan, Tajani stated, "Travelling for tourism today is a right. The way we spend our holidays is a formidable indicator of our quality of life." His spokesman added, "Why should someone from the Mediterranean not be able to travel to Edinburgh in summer for a breath of cool, fresh air; why should someone from Edinburgh not be able to travel to Greece in winter?"

EurActiv, an independent media portal, criticized the article by The Sunday Times as an example of misleading information about the EU to appear in the British press and then picked up by other Anglo-Saxon media and blogs, and Wikipedia. EurActiv stated that "the article on The Sunday Times never quotes the commissioner as having made such a statement. Nevertheless, it pursues the argument under the headline "Brussels decrees holidays as a human right," underlining the alleged "hundreds of millions of pounds" that pursuing the idea would cost taxpayers." Wikipedia was criticized by EurActiv regarding the difficulty that Commissioner Tajani's team had with changing the wrong information on the encyclopedia, and echoed European Commission spokesperson Pia Ahrenkilde Hansen's statement that "ethics in digital communications is definitely a subject which deserves to be addressed."

Chapter 2

KNOWING THE PULSE OF TOURISTS

Research by budget airline Jetstar shows the Japanese want new and realistic experiences after they arrive in the region.

Jetstar will present the findings of extensive research to Tourism Tropical North Queensland members tomorrow.

Airline marketing and public relations head David May will outline the new campaign which is based on one of the most significant pie-ces of Japanese consumer research conducted in recent times.

"We conducted general market research backed up by one-on-one interviews to gain an in-depth understanding of the key drivers of the Japanese consumer and their travel choices, " he said.

"The research shows that, while the Japanese relate very well to Australia, that positive disposition doesn't always translate to visits and suggests we need to repackage Australia and Far North Queensland.

"We need to present new and tangible experiences and images to Japanese consumers in order to revitalise the region's appeal."

Mr May said the campaign would be supported by a multi-million dollar commitment from Jetstar and built on an investment of more than $80 million in marketing support since the airline launched its Japanese services.

"We see real opportunities for the Japanese market," he said.

"We're absolutely on board to work with our local partners which will help ensure Jetstar and the region can capitalise on opportunities the market presents."

The campaign, shot in Cairns in May, will be previewed tomorrow by the local tourism industry before it hits Japan later this month.

"We have been working in partnership with Tourism Tropical North Queensland, Cairns International Airport, Tourism Australia and a host of local businesses to produce a brand new campaign featuring Japanese megastar Becky to reinvigorate the inbound tourism market," Mr May said.

"Jetstar is keen to play a leading role in the Japanese market's recovery.

"That's why we reaffirmed our commitment with the relaunch of our four times weekly Osaka service to build on our daily service to Narita in Tokyo."

In the weeks leading up to the 2010 Olympics in Vancouver, British Columbia (BC), Tourism British Columbia released a new commercial it spent millions of dollars on in order to promote tourism in the province. The fact that most of the world already knew the 2010 winter Olympics were being held there apparently was not enough. The commercial features notable Canadians Michael J. Fox, Sarah McLachlan, Ryan Reynolds, Kim Cattrall, Steve Nash, and Erick McCormack; what it doesn't feature is much ethnic diversity.

There are two versions: the 90-second and the 30-second version. The version most are likely familiar with is the 30-second version. I say that because it is the only version I have personally seen aired on Canadian TV; I wasn't aware the 90-second version even existed until I came across it while searching for the commercial on YouTube. In either case, it is clear the intended target amongst potential tourists are only those as white as the snow featured in the many expensive aerial shots.

What is Tourism British Columbia thinking? Is it that there are aren't PoC out there with money that are worth marketing to as well? Surely, they're not thinking that the only good tourist dollar is a White tourist's dollar, are they? We can't really know what their intention-conscious or subconscious-was in making obviously Caucasian-centric tourism ads, but the result is promo that exclusively targets Whites. Perhaps they didn't feel the need to tout BC's multiculturalism because they didn't feel it was in their interest to do so.

Canada is fairly well known for its multiculturalism; in fact, multiculturalism is protected in section 27 of the Canadian Charter of Rights and Freedoms, which states "This Charter shall be interpreted in a manner consistent with the preservation and enhancement of the multicultural heritage of Canadians." And while Canada does often do well by this declaration, it often has moments where it fails to truly live up to its reputation.

Despite the cultural diversity in urban centers such as Toronto, Montreal and Vancouver, it is still a country where White is considered the norm and this attitude is systematically reflected in our institutions, our culture, our history, and our national self-image. In other words, we like to think of ourselves as a country that is very divers and multicultural, but the truth is we are more ethnocentric than we want to admit. Canada usually jumps at the chance to put our multiculturalism on parade when the world is looking, but the rest of the time-as this Tourism British Columbia ad exemplifies-it's "White as usual."

A bed and breakfast (or B&B) is a small lodging establishment that offers overnight accommodation and breakfast, but usually does not offer other meals. Typically, bed and breakfasts are private homes with fewer than 10 bedrooms available for commercial use.

Generally, guests are accommodated in private bedrooms with private bathrooms, or in a suite of rooms including an en suite bathroom. Some homes have private bedrooms with a bathroom which is shared with other guests. Breakfast is served in the bedroom, a dining room, or the host's kitchen.

B&Bs and guest houses may be operated either as a secondary source of income or a primary occupation. Usually the owners themselves prepare the breakfast and clean the room etc., but some bed and breakfasts hire staff for cleaning or cooking. Although some bed and breakfast owners hire professional staff, a property which hires professional management is usually no longer considered a bed and breakfast, but enters the category of inn or hotel.

Some B&Bs operate in a niche market. Floating bed and breakfasts for example are a concept originating in Seattle in which a boat or houseboat offers B&B accommodation.

REGIONAL DIFFERENCES

Australia

Despite the cultural similarities and a population more than twenty times greater, there are far fewer B&Bs in the whole of Australia than there are in just the South Island of New Zealand.

Since the 1960s the average per capita disposable income of Australians has been greater than that of New Zealanders and this has mitigated the powerful incentive to let out rooms in their homes to travellers. Another factor may be that Australia has, apart from City States such as Singapore, the greatest concentration of city dwellers anywhere on the globe and these cities are amply supplied with budget hotels and motels.

British Isles

B&Bs, and frequently guest houses, are a budget option where owners often take pride in the high service levels, local knowledge and personal touch that they are able to offer.

There tend to be concentrations of B&Bs in seaside towns where, historically, the working classes holidayed such as County

Down, Northern Ireland, and Blackpool, England, and isolated rural areas such as the Highlands of Scotland and Connemara where there is not the year-round concentration of travellers that would sustain an hotel. They are present in most towns and cities, and their numbers vary on trade such as for business travellers and tourists: York and Edinburgh for example both have several hundred establishments known as either B&Bs or guest houses. In very busy areas, B&Bs may display a sign saying "VACANCIES" (rooms available) or "NO VACANCIES", to save both the hosts and potential guests the trouble of them having to enquire within.

Breakfast is usually cooked on demand for the guest and is usually some kind of full breakfast, but some offer a continental breakfast.

In recent years B&Bs in the UK have struggled against budget hotel chains such as Premier Inn and Travelodge. Traditionally, business travellers used B&Bs but many of these clients now tend to stay in budget hotel chains. However, in holiday areas the B&B and guest house still prevail. Unlike the hotel chains, they provide a more comprehensive service and breakfast is included in the price, and some who stay regularly may simply like knowing their hosts.

B&Bs tend to place their bedrooms within three different categories:

- Deluxe: This standard of B&B accommodation in Ireland is considered to be very high and deluxe rooms would be available in high end B&Bs and guesthouse accommodation. Deluxe rooms would often have additional furniture or Jacuzzis in the bathroom. Check the description.
- En-Suite: There is a private bathroom within the bedroom. This will always contain a WC and washbasin, and a shower or bath or both.
- Standard: There is not a bathroom within the bedroom. In this case there will be shared bathroom facilities in another room on the corridor. Usually there will be a washbasin within the room.

Cuba

In Cuba, which opened up to tourism in the 1990s after the financial support of the Soviet Union ended, a form of B&B called casa particular ("private home") became the main form of accommodation outside the tourist resorts.

Israel

In the patio of a guest house in Tamchy, Kyrgyzstan

The Israeli B&B is known as a zimmer (German for room). All over the country, but especially in the north of the country and the Galilee, zimmers have become an alternative to hotels for romantic weekends or family vacations.

Italy

In Italy, regional law regulates B&Bs.

India

In India, the government is promoting the concept of bed & breakfast. The government is doing this to increase tourism, especially keeping in view the expected demand for hotels during the 2010 Commonwealth Games in Delhi. They have classified B&B in 2 categories - Gold & Silver B&B. All B&B will be approved by the Ministry of Tourism who will then categorize it as Gold or Silver based upon the pre-defined criteria.

Kyrgyzstan

The tourism industry in Kyrgyzstan includes some B&Bs. One group, called CBT, organises homestays with people who own homes and rent rooms by the night. They help tourists and travelers in Kyrgyzstan find places to stay.

Pakistan

The trend of B&Bs in Pakistan is quite widespread. Popular resorts like Murree, which attract many tourists from different parts of the country, have a number of such resthouses. The expenses can vary, depending on the quality of facilites. Most bed and breakfast facilities tend to expediently cater to families, given the high level of group tourism, and offer suitable overnight lodging.

New Zealand

A Centre of New Zealand Bed and Breakfast

As in the USA, bed and breakfasts in New Zealand tend to be more expensive than motels and often feature historic homes and furnished bedrooms at a commensurate price.

North America

Many B&Bs in North America try to create a historical ambiance, with old properties turned into guesthouses decorated with antique furniture. For example, the Holladay House in Orange, Virginia is an 1830s Federal-style brick building that has been converted into a bed and breakfast. In the last ten years, B&B and Inn owners have been launching upscale amenities to improve business and move "up-market." It is not uncommon now to find free wireless Internet access, free parking, spa services, or nightly wine and cheese hours. Due to the need to stay competitive with the rest of the lodging industry, larger bed and breakfast inns have expanded to offer wedding services, business conference facilities, and meeting spaces as well as many other services a large hotel might offer.

The custom of opening one's home to travellers dates back the earliest day of Colonial America. Lodging establishments were few and far between in the 1700s, and apart from a limited number of coaching inns (a few of which survive as inns today), wayfarers relied on the kindness of strangers to provide a bed for the night. Hotels became more common with the advent of the railroad, and later, the automobile, and most towns had at least one prominent hotel.

During the Great Depression, tourist homes provided an economic advantage to both the traveller and the host. Driving through town (no Interstates then), travellers stopped at houses with signs reading Tourists or Guests, indicating that travellers could rent a room for the night for about $2. The money generated needed income for the home owner and saved money for the traveller.

After World War II, middle-class Americans began travelling in Europe in large numbers, many experiencing the European-style B&Bs (Zimmer frei in Germany, chambres d'hotes in France) for the first time. Some were inspired to open B&Bs in the U.S.; tourist home owners updated their properties as B&Bs. The interest in B&Bs coincided with an increasing interest in historic preservation, spurred by the U.S. Bicentennial in 1976 and assisted by two crucial pieces of legislation: the National Historic Preservation Act of 1966, and the Tax Reform Act of 1976, which provided tax incentives for the restoration and reuse of historic structures.

Through the 1980s and 1990s, B&Bs increased rapidly in numbers and evolved from homestay B&Bs with shared baths and a simple furnishings to beautifully renovated historic mansions with luxurious décor and amenities. The next big change started in the mid 1990s when the Internet became a major marketing force, making it affordable for innkeepers to promote their properties worldwide. Email marketing, in particular, serves as a useful tool for the Bed & Breakfast industry, for it proactively builds relationships with the existing guests after their stay. This helps increase the likelihood for more repeat bookings and also guest referrals in the future. At present, travellers research and book B&B online, checking out detailed photos, videos, and reviews. B&Bs are found in all states, in major cities and remote rural areas, occupying everything from modest cottages to opulent mansions, and in restored structures from schools to cabooses to churches.

Spain

In Spain, B&Bs are often run by people who place personal or family needs ahead of wealth and profit maximization. The business attracts numerous entrepreneurs with predominantly lifestyle motives, yet challenges them in specific ways. Spain does not have a B&B culture like Great Britain. As anything "modern" rules, locals usually shake their head at tourists visiting B&Bs when they could stay at a "proper hotel" for the same money or less.

A study of the years 1997-2000, using a sample of 1131 Spanish firms, suggests that marketing must be done over the medium to long term to be effective.

Regulations

Regulations and laws vary considerably between jurisdictions both in content and extent and in enforcement.

The most common regulations B&Bs must follow pertain to safety. They are usually required by local and national ordinances to have fire resistance, a sufficient fire escape plan in place, and smoke detectors in each guest room. Kitchens and equipment used to serve meals are also often required to be monitored for hygienic operation, but there are significant national and local differences.

In Hawaii, it is illegal to open a new bed & breakfast on Oahu as of 1989. The reason for the moratorium is to force home owners with extra room to rent out their extra space to low income residents who otherwise cannot afford housing on crowded Oahu.

Many inns and bed and breakfasts are members of professional associations. There are international, national, regional, and local associations, all of which provide services to both their members and the travelling public. Many require their members to meet specific standards of quality, while others simply require a lodging establishment to pay dues. These associations also facilitate marketing of the individual B&Bs and provide a stamp of approval that the business in question is reputable.

While various local governments have regulations and inspect lodging establishments for health and safety issues, membership in a state/provincial/national bed and breakfast association can indicate a higher standard of hospitality. Associations sometimes review their members' properties and tend to have additional standards of care.

In the US for example, each state has an innkeeping association (usually non-profit) that exists to promote the industry and tourism. However, many state associations, have rigorous inspection criteria that often exceed government requirements for safety and cleanliness.

In Australia, the industry is represented by the Bed & Breakfast, Farmstay and Accommodation Australia Ltd (BBFAA).

Organizations such as the Automobile Association also provide periodical inspections of B&B inns.

In the British Isles the national approval boards set up by governments are far more stringent than others,while in Ireland there is an association that will only use the national tourist board's approved members (Almara Accommodations Dublin)

STUDIES

Tourism Queensland Study

In January 2003 Tourism Queensland conducted a review of current research to gain a better understanding of the Bed & Breakfast (B&B) market:

- Key needs that must be met for people staying at bed and breakfast style accommodation include: pampering and personalised service in an attractive location in an attractive house, opposed to more 'standard' hotelrooms.

  The following attributes are also appealing:

- Homely or wholesome atmosphere (older segments) or luxurious/heritage surrounds
- Home style meals
- Area for conversing with other guests
- Ability to tap into local knowledge of attractions and activities in local area.

Guests at B&Bs were asked to identify the features and factors which motivated them to choose the establishment they were staying at. The friendliness of the host was the most important factor, followed by easy access to other places, the site being the most appealing place in the region. Usually B & B´s are privately owned, and therefor very different from standard commercial hotels.

Bed & Breakfasts provide mutual benefits for both the visitor and the operator. Visitors have the opportunity for a relaxing break in a homely environment. Operators have the opportunity to develop a profitable business, make new friends and contacts, understand the cultures andlifestyles of others, and to educate guests about their way of life.

Income and leisure time have changed so that shorter breaks with greater choice of leisure activities are sought. Changing work patterns have increased the popularity of shorter breaks that minimize the absence from work and the effect of absences on workflow and involvement. Bed & Breakfast holidays tend to be short break holidays and could benefit from the increased popularity of short breaks, sought by people who aim for authenticity and personal service."

MICHIGAN STATE UNIVERSITY STUDY

According to a study by Michigan State University:

- The profile of B&B guests confirms widely held impressions that this is a middle-aged, well-educated, (moderately) high income, professional market. On the last reported B&B trip, couples comprised two thirds of the travel parties.

Eighty-two percent of those sampled are married, and about half (44 percent) have children living at home. Average age for a travel party (respondent and spouse/partner ages are merged) is 40 years, with 60 percent under this age. This indicates that many B&B guests are at a mid-point in the traditional family cycle, when raising children is a primary activity. Newlyweds and "empty nesters" account for a smaller proportion. In fact, only 9 percent of the market is attributed to adults over 59 years of age.

Education levels are high, with the largest response category being completion of a college degree (31 percent). In addition, another one third had some graduate school or an advanced degree. It follows that the occupational profile is dominated by professionals and managers. Note that several categories such as business, health, education, and science are large enough for B&B's to consider promotion aimed specifically at these segments.

The unique touches that distinguish a B&B are clearly a primary reason for selecting this lodging option. Words like "charm," ambience," "quaintness," and "atmosphere" were often used by respondents to describe this intangible appeal. The importance of the "getaway" aspect demonstrates that B&B's have been well positioned to take advantage of shorter, more frequent weekend trips preferred by many two-income families. The lure of B&B's as a more personal alternative to the standard hotel/motel experience was reconfirmed by the 10 percent who called this the single most important reason for staying at a B&B, the most frequent response to this open-ended question.

Customers were for the most part satisfied with their most recent B&B experience, with 80 percent giving the experience an .. excellent" rating and another 17 percent calling it "good." Over 90 percent would both consider a return visit and recommend the B&B to friends and family."

According to this study, many bed and breakfast visitors make use of evaluations, given by other guests. This system of independent reviews is one of the fastest growing consumer content oriented sites on the net.

ComScore study

Another study suggests that people trust online reviews posted by previous guests:

" People are willing to pay up to 99 percent more for services after reading positive online reviews about them, according to new research.

The study, conducted in October by comScore and The Kelsey Group, found that online, consumer-created reviews have a big impact on prospective buyers. The researchers said 24 percent of those who eventually pay for local services -- such as restaurants, bed & breakfasts and automotive shops -- read online reviews before making a choice.

The study showed consumers were so trusting of online reviews, they were willing to pay at least 20 percent, and up to 99 percent, more if a company was rated excellent or five-star than if a business received a good, or four-star, rating. The study was based on 2,078 survey respondents, including 508 who used online consumer reviews.

Professional critics, and owners of companies that receive less-than-excellent online reviews by laypersons, might question the ability of regular people to adequately judge a service. However, the comScore/Kelsey Group study found that 90 percent of the people who trusted consumer-written reviews found the critiques to be accurate. In fact, noted the researchers, "reviews generated by fellow consumers had a greater influence than those generated by professionals."

The study included specific bed & breakfasts among others services. At least 75 percent of those using online reviews for nearly every category of business included in the study said the amateur field reports significantly impacted their decision. Eighty-seven percent of those in search of hotels said the reviews played a big part in their choice.

The take-away message for service providers, according to a statement issued by The Kelsey Group's research director, Steve Marshall: "With such a large percentage of review users subsequently purchasing, it's vital that local service providers have a positive presence on these review sites."

The fact that one-in-four of those contacted said they use reviews should come as good news for those in the online consumer review space, said Brian Jurutka, senior director at comScore Marketing Solutions. "That's a sizeable chunk," he said. "This helps them in having discussions with folks looking to advertise; it says a sizeable portion of the online population is going to be visiting these sites." "

JOURNAL OF TRAVEL RESEARCH STUDY

A study by the Journal of Travel Research stated:

" While the hedonic price model has been used to evaluate willingness to pay in a variety of markets, its use in the tourism industry is limited. This research note highlights the usefulness of the hedonic price technique in this industry by evaluating willingness to pay for specific characteristics of bed and breakfast accommodations.

Heterogeneity in price and amenities offered by bed and breakfast accommodations enables us to generate estimates of willingness to pay for specific characteristics. Using data on price and amenities collected from bed and breakfast accommodations, the findings show a willingness to pay for specific characteristics such as sunny balconies, a five star Champagne breakfast, and a room furnished with antique treasures... "

Prince Edward Island study

A 2007 Study on Prince Edward Island

"The vast majority of visitors to B & B are pleasure travellers. The most important reasons why travellers choose a B & B are personalised service and hospitality, price and value ratio, physical element, atmosphere, image and location."

TIME Magazine

According to TIME magazine:

> Americans have a wide array of lodgings to choose from when they take a vacation: high-rise hotels, rustic resorts, motels by the bay. Yet more and more people are flocking to bed-and-breakfast inns, the most old-fashioned homes away from home. Just 20 years ago, there were only 1,000 B and Bs, as they are nicknamed, scattered throughout the country. Today there are more than 28,000 serving more than 50 million guests each year.

What's the appeal? Bed-and-breakfasts, often situated in elegant, historic homes, tap into everyone's fantasy of living another life. Many have been lovingly renovated with period decorations, inviting visitors to step back in time. Take a look at this popular arty one in Spain for example: www.valenciamansion.com . Others carry a theme throughout the house. Since on average they have only seven or eight rooms, they offer peace and quiet, a rare commodity in the average home.

The hosts, who nearly always live on the premises, provide plenty of coddling. They will recommend local attractions, help with dinner reservations, often provide an afternoon tea or glass of sherry--and, yes, prepare a delicious homemade breakfast.

Prices at bed-and-breakfasts, which average $104 to $133 a night, depending on the region, rival the rates of good hotels. While some 10,000 B and Bs are private homes in which the owners offer a room or two, most are serious businesses, complete with websites and toll-free numbers.

The clientele tends to be couples, most of them affluent and well educated. Most are tourists or people who are in town to visit family or to celebrate a special occasion. Bed-and-breakfasts are popular with many foreign travelers, mostly from Britain, Germany, Canada, France and Australia, who have grown up going to B and Bs in their own countries.

How to Tap Tourist Market?

The travel and tourism industry is the third largest employer in the United States, supporting over 5.85 million travel-related jobs. Foreign and domestic visitors traveling in the United States generate over $327 billion in tourism revenues in a year, making travel and tourism the third largest retail sales industry.* The percent of the total tourist dollar being spent on shopping is on the rise. Marketing an area's specialties including crafts and other products can be one way to take advantage of this trend and help to diversity the economic base of a rural area or community.

National Travel and Tourism Awareness Council

If you target the tourist market, what types of products appeal to people who take part in different tourist activities? Are handcrafted items of interest to tourists?

How can you improve existing marketing strategies?

To find answers to these questions, a research team from Iowa, Minnesota, and Nebraska, gathered information from more than 1400 individuals on ways to improve the marketing of crafts and other products to tourists. Participants included tourists, craft producers, and retailers who sell crafts. Much of what tourists told us about their travel interests and activities has implications for tourist communities, tourist attractions, and hospitality services as well as for craft producers and retailers. Here are the major research findings and suggestions for you to consider.

Meet The Tourists

We started by getting to know the tourists in this project in a general way---their trips to our states, travel interests, shopping activities, and some background information. It's helpful to know about tourists in a general way, especially if your business or community appeals to a wide variety of tourists. This information can help you assess your responsiveness to tourists' interests and evaluate your current services and products.

Tourists Enjoyed Their Visits

Travelers to all three states were satisfied withtheir visits, in most cases, a first trip to the state. In fact, they gave higher marks to the state as a tourist attraction than did the craft producers and retailers from that state. Most tourists in our study were on vacation (62%) or were visiting family and friends (25%). They traveled in a party of 3 to 4 persons, They stayed in the state for an average of seven days; half stayed for five days or less.

Tourists Shop

Shopping is an important activity for tourists. After meals and lodging they report spending most money on:

- T-shirts, sweatshirts, and other clothes with a name or design representing the location or attraction

- Crafts

- Local food products (not meals)

Almost 70% buy gifts ahead of time for holidays, birthdays, and similar events. See the Shopping chart on page 3 for more information on how tourists spend money when they travel. Craft buying by tourists The tourists in our study told us they look for crafts to use and display in their home. They also enjoy seasonal and holiday items. Their favorite craft medium is wood, followed by nature materials and fabric.

How do Tourists Find Places to Buy Crafts?

Over 50% of the tourists used these sources to find crafts in a community or within the state: tourist brochures or state travel packets; local shops; magazines or newspaper articles; travel magazines and guide books; people who have been there before; directory or map of art or craft locations or events; information at the hotel, either written or from hotel personnel; local residents; and ads in local papers. They made less use of travel agents, tour guides, or telephone books for this information.

Where do Tourists Shop for Crafts?

Tourists are most likely to shop for crafts at craft fairs and festivals, craft shops, and gift shops carrying both crafts and other types of gift products. Many enjoy shopping in a historic house typical of the region or shop with a rustic appearance.

How Much do Tourists Spend on a Craft Item?

That depends on the person receiving it. The tourists in our study tend to spend:

- $20-30 for a craft item for themselves, a close friend, or relative

- $10-20 on a craft item meant for other adults and children on their gift list (including people tending plants and mail while they are away)

- $5-10 on token gifts for coworkers.

Displays, orderliness, and written information help sell crafts While tourists find a large selection of crafts filling every nook and cranny of a shop is desirable, they appreciate neatly arranged displays to bring a sense of order. Displays featuring ways to use and display crafts in the home help sell crafts since some tourists want assistance visualizing ways to use crafts in their homes. Tourists want written information on care, safety, materials used, and ways to use the craft items.

Sales personnel contribute to the ideal shopping environment Tourists value sales personnel who let them browse, who initiate pleasant conversation, and who can provide information about the craft producer and craft technique. Shopping, an important tourist activity Tourists expect to shop when they travel. This chart shows: 1) the products they generally buy, and 2) categories on which they spend the most money. Retailers appealing to tourists might use this information to plan merchandise assortments, promotional activities, and pricing strategies. Communities might also use this information to help evaluate the mix of businesses serving tourist needs in their towns.

Products Tourists Generally Buy	(% of tourists buying)
Postcards and booklets about sites visited	72%.
T-shirts, sweatshirts, other clothes with name or picture of location or attraction	68%
Crafts	61%
Local food products (not meals)	52%
Books about area, state, people, history, or attractions	40%
Items they can add to a collection	35%
Mementos of location or attraction (pens, bumper stickers, balloons, key chains)	32%
Antiques	26%

Categories on which Tourists Spend the Most Money	(% of tourists spending most money on the category)
T-shirts, sweatshirts, other clothes with	

name or pictureof location or attraction	34%
Crafts	19%
Local food products (not meals)	10%
Antiques	9%
Items they can add to a collection	8%
Books about area, state, people, history, or attractions	7%
Postcards and booklets about sites visited	5%
Mementos of location or attraction (pens, bumper stickers, balloons, key chains)	4%
Other	4%

Four Specialized Tourist Styles Match

By choice or by necessity, many communities, especially rural ones, have focused their tourist attractions and other supporting businesses and services on a limited range of activities. Knowing as much as possible about the interests of travelers to specialized tourist areas can help you invest your time and money in efforts that appeal to your visitors and result in increased profit for your business and community.

So, in addition to studying the tourists in a general way, we identified four specialized tourism styles among the tourists. People in each tourism style enjoyed similar travel activities and shopping opportunities. They reacted in similar ways to words describing craft themes and types of craft producers. They used similar criteria when they bought crafts. A tourist might adopt more than one of these tourism styles depending on where she or he is traveling and what's available.

Ethnic, Arts, and People Style

Ethnic, Arts, and People tourists are actively involved in their tourism. They immerse themselves in the community. For them, tourism is an opportunity for education and personal development. It's a time for experiencing authenticity in a community and its way of life.

They actively:

- Visit ethnic communities
- Participate in community festivals
- Visit art galleries and museums
- Attend concerts and the theater
- Interact with local residents

Products they buy:

- Crafts
- Local food products (does not include meals)
- Antiques Books about the area they are visiting

Craft preferences:

They are attracted to timeless crafts such as:

- Ethnic crafts
- Folk art
- Designer crafts
- Traditional crafts of the region

Specifically they look for.

- Crafts that can be used in the home
- Jewelry
- Crafts to add to their collections

Criteria for selecting crafts:

- Appealing color, design, and quality workmanship
- Items that are unique and represent new ideas
- Crafts made by well-known artisans who sign their work

Sources for finding crafts:

- Printed materials such as directories or maps of

Craftperson's Studios

- Brochures at museums
- Suggestions from local residents and shops

Places they shop for crafts:

- Art gallery or museum shops
- Antique shops
- Booths at craft fairs, festivals, bazaars, and flea markets
- Craftperson's studio or workshop

Preferred craft shopping environment:

- Shops with rustic appearance
- Historic houses
- Artisans demonstrating their work

History and Parks Style

The History and Parks tourists are introspective. They devote time to enjoying scenery, contemplating a sense of place, reflecting on the past, and photographing the experience. They take time to plan their trips.

They visit:

- Historic sites and homes
- Museums
- Recreated villages that depict a past way of life
- Gardens
- State and national parks

Products they buy:

- Crafts
- Postcards
- Books about the area and its history

- Local food products
- Items to add to their collections

Craft preferences:

They like crafts with these themes:

- Regional
- Historic
- Ethnic
- Nature
- Country
- Western

They look especially for crafts they can display in their homes.

Criteria for selecting crafts:

- Appealing color, design, and quality workmanship
- Clever ideas
- Can display in the home
- Easy care
- Easy to pack
- Includes the name or theme related to site

Sources for finding crafts:

- Travel packets from state tourism bureaus prior to a trip
- Materials available at tourist sites

Places they shop for crafts:

- Parks and tourist sites
- Theme parks
- Tourist visitor centers
- Highway or rest stops
- Craft shops and gift shops

- Craft fairs, festivals, bazaars, and flea markets
- Craftperson's studio or workshop
- Art gallery or museum shop

Four common tourist sites

As you examine these tourism styles consider:

- How do these styles relate to your community, attraction, shop or craft product?

- What kinds of services could you emphasize to please these visitors?

- Do their interests suggest products that you could add to your selection?

- How can you use this information to promote your enterprise or products?

- Does this information give you ideas for specific words to use in your signage, ads, and other written information?

- How do these styles help you fine-tune the community image you want to portray to visitors?

Active Outdoor Style

Active Outdoor tourists are outdoor enthusiasts who vigorously enjoy parks and nature areas.

They actively:

- Hike and backpack
- Camp
- Fish
- Sail and boat
- Hunt
- Swim
- Ski
- Play tennis or golf

Products they buy:

- T-shirts and sweatshirts with a name or design related to the location

Craft preferences:

Crafts are not a major focus. When they do select crafts they prefer products made from nature materials such as grasses, corn husks, pine cones, dried flowers, and stone.

These themes are appealing:

- Rural
- Western
- Recreation
- Folk art
- Traditional themes

Criteria for selecting crafts:

- Can display in their homes
- Humor
- Name or design related to the location
- Made by well-known craftperson
- Is signed, marked, or a limited edition

Places they shop for crafts:

- General store serving a resort or camping area
- Gas station or convenience store
- Parks or recreation gift shop

Urban Entertainment Style

Urban Entertainment tourists visit cities where they are constantly on the go, day and night. Social interaction is important to these travellers. Many use packaged tours. These are young men and women with higher incomes. They travel extensively in the U.S.

They enthusiastically:

- "Shop 'til they drop."
- Attend professional sports events
- Visit recreational theme parks
- Go dancing and nightclubbing

Products they buy:

They look for products with the name or design representing their vacation location.

They buy:

- T-shirts and sweatshirts
- Souvenir items such as pens, bumper stickers, and key chains
- Crafts

Craft preferences:

They prefer general craft themes such as:

- Handicrafts
- Designer crafts
- Contemporary crafts
- Western themes

They look specifically for crafts with visual impact:

- Crafts to display in their homes
- Seasonal or holiday decorations
- Clothes, accessories, or jewelry to wear Criteria for selecting crafts:
- Ease of care and cleaning
- Items that are new, innovative, limited edition, signed
- Humor
- Name or design related to the location or attraction

Sources for finding crafts:

- Hotel staff
- Printed materials in hotel rooms or at hotel desks

Places they shop for crafts:

- They shop everywhere:
- Hotels and restaurants
- Theme parks
- Sports centers
- Visitor centers
- Gas stations
- Clothing and accessory boutiques
- Craftperson's studio or workshop

They are attracted to shops with either crowded or modern appearances.

Successful craft producers tap into the tourist market. Perhaps you, like the craft producers in our study, want to increase your sales to tourists. Knowing how successful craft producers market their work can help you review your business practices with an eye to tourists and profit. In our study, success was measured by the craft producer's gross income, percent contributed to household income, years in business, and self evaluation of their own success.

Successful craft producers promoted themselves and their products by:

- providing business cards and hang tags
- signing their work
- using a logo
- offering limited edition information
- providing written biographical data

Successful craft producers used more wholesale channels, including:

- direct sale to retailers
- trade/wholesale shows
- selling to retailers at craft fairs
- sales representatives
- mail order ads to retailers

Higher income producers ($20,000 and over):

- Worked an average of 55 hours per week, considerably more than those in lower income groups;

- Concentrated on a particular medium or technique, offering fewer types of items in their product line;

- Identified themselves as: artist, artist/craftsman, and designer/craftsman. Producers in the lower income group called themselves artisan, craftsman, folk artist, and handicrafter;

- Were 66.7% male. Men contributed a higher percentage to household income. On average, their most expensive items were 4 times the price of those of women; their least expensive items were twice the price of those of women.

If you wish to increase your income:

- Review your promotional practices;

- Target communities, attractions, shops, and craft fairs serving the tourism styles most compatible with your products;

- Target the wholesale market place to get your products to tourist communities;

- Review your price structure;

- Review the type of product you produce in relation to tourist demand;

- Continue to develop your capacity to be original, create your own designs;

- Stay abreast of the number of people producing crafts similar to yours;

- Review your professional practices and work habits;

- Stay alert to tourist interests. See general trends in "Retailers' strategies for marketing crafts to tourists," later in article. Check with retailers selling your products about tourist interests in their location.

Retailers' strategies for marketing crafts to tourists. Identifying a target market may be difficult for retailers wanting to cater to both local residents and tourists. Retailers cannot necessarily apply knowledge of their local customers' purchasing habits to tourists. Knowing what retailers in tourist areas are doing to market crafts can help you review your business plan with the tourist market in mind. Here are some questions to ask yourself.

1. Do you know your area's tourist resources?

Retailers viewed tourism as important to the local area and to the state's economy. Attracting more tourists was seen as a good idea. However, retailers did not necessarily view their state as a tourist state or interesting for tourists. Nor did they have an understanding of their role with tourists.

Feelings about the attractiveness or pull of their state are communicated by retailers in direct contact with tourists. Retailers knowledgeable about the resources, history, and products of their area are better able to serve tourists and market products to tourists.

2. Do current inventories meet tourists' demands?

The reported craft supply did not always meet the perceived demand of tourists.

Tourists wanted more of these craft items than they found available:

- leather items
- glass items
- handcrafted toys

- jewelry
- clothing
- functional crafts for use in the home

Retailers appeared to carry more of these craft items than tourists indicated they were likely to buy:

- crafts in these media: fabric, paint, and paper
- crafts to display in the home

When selecting their craft inventory, retailers considered criteria that were similar to those used by tourists.

Those were appealing design and color, quality of workmanship, price, and newness or innovation.

Retailers are encouraged to explore whether tourists associate a particular craft with a local historic site, ethnic festival, or attraction. Most retailers perceived that tourists traveling through their state did not associate a particular type of craft with the state; however, tourists tend to view crafts and other objects purchased during travel as having symbolic value. These products may be among tourists' most valued possessions as reminders of their travel experiences.

3. What types of advertisements, promotion, and hours attract tourists?

Retailers were most likely to use visual displays of the crafts and direct customer contact as selling techniques. Advertising was done primarily through print media. Over half of the retailers held special events to promote craft sales, such as open houses, special shows, seasonal events, and in-house classes or demonstrations. Retailers did not seem to rely on brochures for advertising, although tourists preferred brochures for information on crafts.

Careful analysis of activities of tourists in the area and the enroute tourists may reflect a seasonal pattern or suggest days and hours when tourists want to shop. Although most retailers reported that they were open all year for business, their busiest months were June through August and November and December. January through March were the slowest months for selling crafts. Tourist departments, travel centers, lodging and resort facilities, and Chambers of Commerce might provide additional insight on general tourist patterns.

4. What will give you the edge with tourists?

Retailers need to think about the possibility of tourists as a targeted consumer group. Target marketing, used in conjunction with the four tourism styles we identified, has potential for retailers who would like to increase their sales to tourists. See pages 4 and 5 for descriptions of the four tourism styles: Ethnic, Arts, and People style; History and Parks style; Active Outdoor style; and Urban Entertainment Style.

Many tourists value "uniqueness" in the crafts they select and retailers tended to focus on the uniqueness or novelty of their products. However, uniqueness alone may not be enough if the product isn't right for the target market.

Craft Producer and Retailer Relationships

A strong working relationship between the craft producer and the retailer can result in increased profits for both parties. The relationship can be strengthened by a better understanding of how they make initial contacts with one another, what incentives they offer, how they work together on pricing, and what problems they encounter in the relationship.

Making Contacts

Craft producers typically contact retailers directly. They learn about retailers through other craft producers and by contacts at fairs and shows.

Incentives

Craft retailers offered these incentives to producers:

- special care of the product and safe-guards to prevent theft and damage

- quick payment
- knowledgeable sales help

Craft producers looked for retailers who offered quick payment, location in a tourist area, adequate space to display their work, and a favorable percentage of the consignment price.

Craft producers provided these incentives to retailers:

- volume discounts
- deferred payments
- exclusivity of product line
- easy exchange of items

Retailers wanted more information about the craft producer and the product.

PURCHASING AND PRICING

- Most retailers purchased crafts on a wholesale and/or consignment basis.
- Retailers carried craft items an average of six months.
- Over half the retailers returned 70 to 80 percent of the retail price to consignor.
- Most retailers worked in conjunction with the craftperson to set the retail price for consignment.
- Most retailers determined on the wholesale price of crafts according to the craft based on past selling history.

PROBLEMS

Retailers identified problems with craft producers related to:

- overpriced products
- unsteady source of supply from season to season

Craft producers identified problem with retailers such as:

- retailers slow to pay

- taking too large a percentage on consignment
- keeping poor records
- going out of business
- lost or stolen items

Recommendations to craft producers

- Create incentives for retailers with volume discount, deferred payments, exclusivity of product line, and easy exchange of items.

- Evaluate your ability to produce products in relationship to the amount of orders accepted.

- Explain your wholesale price to retailers, in terms related to design, quality, innovativeness, and timeliness.

- Provide retailers with information about yourself and your product. Sign your work. Consider producing limited editions.

- Discuss with the retailer your availability for demonstrations, receptions, and special showings.

- Work with craft retailers as to the best way to display and/or demonstrate your products.

Recommendations to retailers

- Develop a consistent pay schedule and keep producers informed of any changes.

- Explain carefully your process for consigning and pricing items.

- Evaluate your methods of bookkeeping for efficiency and accuracy related to inventory control and payment.

- Review and improve precautions to prevent loss, theft, and damage to items.

Suggestions for increasing your share of the tourist market Our research findings about tourists' travel and shopping interests form the basis for these suggestions. Tourists enjoy travel as a total experience; therefore, community-wide cooperation is necessary to take advantage of the strong link between what tourists like to do and what they like to buy. Consider your business and your goals for taping the tourist market as you decide which of these suggestions offer the greatest potential benefit for you.

KNOW YOUR TOURISTS

How can you learn about tourists and use that information to your advantage---and theirs? Consider these ideas as a community or as an individual business operator.

- Listen to tourists talk about your community to understand why they find it so interesting.

- Review the four tourism styles (see pages 4 and 5) and determine which types are most likely to visit your community.

- Evaluate the services and products in your community to see if they correspond with interests of the tourists most likely to visit.

- Identify new businesses or services to expand the experience of tourists. For example, if your community has an ethnic heritage or annual festival, could you organize ways for visitors to interact with local residents via home visits for coffee or dinner?

- If your community does not have gift or craft shops, consider ways to satisfy tourists' desires to shop such as selling crafts and other products in general stores, gas stations, and convenience stores.

- Consider whether your merchandise "fits" the types of tourists your community attracts. Examples:

1. BOOKS ON TRADITIONAL CRAFTS AND CRAFT PRODUCERS FOR

- Historic and Parks and Ethnic, Arts, and People tourists;

2. FILM OR BLANK VIDEOTAPE FOR HISTORIC AND PARKS TOURISTS

Evaluate your craft product line, your promotion methods, and pricing strategies. Consider:

1. Producing or carrying items for which perceived tourist demand exceeds availability;

2. Including popular gift price ranges - $5-10, $10-20, and $20-30;

3. Localizing products by incorporating a name or design motif that is related to the attraction or location.

Services for Tourists

A customer service orientation is one of the most important strategies you can employ among businesses, tourist attractions, and residents to enhance tourists' experiences in your community.

- Increase the customer service orientation of your sales personnel.

1. Encourage them to engage customers in friendly conversation, at the same time being alert to when customers want to browse alone;

2. Provide training so sales personnel can explain craft techniques, talk about craft producers, and suggest ways to use and display crafts at home;

3. Alert them to items that make good gifts and to the attributes (both aesthetic and practical) that make the items appealing.

- Consider value added services which make the purchasing process easier for tourists. These include services like gift wrap, shipping, monogramming, and acceptance of credit cards.

- Provide written information for tourists on care, safety, and use of crafts; materials used to produce the craft, particularly those of local origin; history or tradition of the craft; and information on the craft producer.

- Let tourists know if crafts are signed, marked, or in limited edition.

- Display crafts to show a variety of ways to use and display them at home. For example, display clay pitchers to illustrate multiple uses: to serve lemonade, to hold flowers, and to add to a grouping of decorative items.

- Periodically change in-store visual displays and promotional materials to reflect new trends.

Tourism as a community-wide venture: Planning and promotion. How can your community work together to help visitors enjoy spending time---and money---in your community? Being involved in your community's tourism organization is one way you can help this happen.

- Seek representation from all aspects of your community. Don't overlook retailers, craft producers, gas station operators, residents, and others who come in contact with tourists.

- Identify the local attractions, products, and crafts that make your community or area unique.

- Plan advertising and promotional efforts around the target tourism styles.

- Appeal to tourists through signs and promotional materials by using terms tourists use to describe desirable themes: Western, designer, etc. Note differences among tourism styles.

- Become well-known in your community so community businesses and residents can promote your business.

- Plan strategies to promote attractions, crafts, and other local products and services in a cooperative way.

1. Develop a list of local craft producers and producers of specialized local products.

2. Develop an active referral system among the community's businesses and attractions to market what your community has to offer to tourists. Exchange supplies of brochures, business cards, etc. to distribute to visitors.

3. Develop cooperative displays among businesses, at tourist attractions, or in public display areas combining items that your target tourists often buy. For example, for Ethnic, Arts, and People tourists combine crafts, local foods, antiques, and books about the area.

- Publicize communities, crafts, and other specialty products in places tourists look for information, e.g. tourist brochures, state tourism packets, magazine and newspaper articles, travel magazines and guidebooks, hotels and restaurants.

- Review advertising opportunities in local newspapers and in tourist brochures, magazines, and guidebooks.

Expand Hospitality Training

- Hospitality training can build awareness about an area's specialty products and crafts as well as inform participants about attractions and teach skills for assisting visitors. Potential participants include anyone in the community who has contact with tourists--employees and managers/owners of restaurants, hotels, B&Bs, shops, gas stations, tourist attractions, other local businesses, and local residents.

- To help mold hospitality training to the needs of your community, assess retailers, craft producers, hospitality services, other businesses, community organizations, and residents on their:

1. Attitudes toward their community as an interesting place to visit;
2. Knowledge about local attractions, resources, craft producers, local products, and services of interest to tourists.

- In your hospitality training include information about the community's ethnic background and traditions, crafts and craft producers, local foods, antiques.

Research details

Three mail surveys were developed for craft producers, craft retailers, and tourists. Survey respondents included 377 craft producers, 373 retailers, and 740 tourists.

Crafts were defined as items that were: handmade, not made in a factory; items made with attention to materials, design, and workmanship. and items that could be useful or decorative. Examples of craft items included weavings, quilts, pottery, tole painting, corn husk dolls, and wood carvings.

Craft Producers

Names of craft producers were drawn from a pool of names collected from art fair organizations, craft organizations, state arts councils, and county Extension agents. Only those craft producers who were currently making and selling crafts and who had been producing crafts to sell to others for more than two years are reported in these findings.

Seventy-seven percent of the craft producers surveyed were female and 23% were male.

The average craft producer:

- 47 years old
- in a rural community
- high school or post-high school education
- in business about 9 years
- contributed about 25% to the household's total income.

The primary media used by craftpersons, in order, were:

wood, fabric, and clay. Most said they produced items for display or use in the home.

Most common methods used to sell crafts:

- Art and craft fairs - 80% of the craft producers
- Own home or shop - 62%
- Consignment selling - 44%
- Wholesaling to retailers - 28%

Seventy-four percent of the craftpersons earned under $10,000. Yet, only 10% were interested in taking another job if one became available. About 45% had another job in addition to their craft business.

Craft Retailers

Names of the craft retailers were obtained from lists of gift shops, state parks and welcome center facilities having gift shops, and from names of craft retailers supplied by county Extension agents in the three states. To be eligible for participation, the retailer had to be in business for one year, carry handmade craft merchandise, have some tourist consumers, and be located near, or on the way to, a tourist area or attraction.

The typical retailer surveyed was the sole owner of a gift shop in a community with a population under 10,000. About half (46%) reported total sales volume of less than $15,000/year.

Tourists

The tourists were drawn from a list of individuals who had requested travel information from the tourism bureaus of Minnesota, Nebraska, or Iowa and had visited the state in the previous year. A "tourist" was defined as a person who is away from home on non-routine travel. The travel might be for the purpose of a vacation, business, attending a convention, or visiting family or friends. The person in the household making the majority of the craft, gift, and souvenir purchases answered the questions.

Sixty-seven percent and 33% male. Over 40% came from towns with populations under 10,000. Only 16% came from cities of 250,000 and over. They represented a wide range of income and education levels. Tourists to all three states were very similar in their responses.

The typical respondent:

- a 45-year-old woman
- education beyond high school
- household income over $30,000
- from community with population under 50,000
- had visited 25 other states and three foreign countries.

For more information: Contact your county Extension office for more assistance. The following videotapes may be available in your state:

CHAPTER 3

WHAT IS CREATIVE IN CREATIVE TOURISM?

The creative tourism is a form of cultural tourism - it counts on cultural assets to attract travelers to a destination. It is also a form of creative community's development - by stimulating the creative industries from outside, the local economy improves beyond the profits from tourism.

On the other side, the business model for creative tourism defers radically from the business model of conventional cultural tourism. First, it is based on a different resources. Cultural tourism is focused on iconic buildings, mega events (festivals, etc.), strong presence of historic heritage, vibrant cultural life at a destination and limited famous geographies (Italy, France, Spain, Egypt, England, etc.).

Creative tourism demand is related to the need for learning and experiencing the creative process - from textiles weaving in the Mapuche regions of Chile to icon-painting in Russia. In some outbound markets, like the USA, the demand is driven in strong traditions and proliferation of hobbies and craft making. And because the creative tourism doesn't need impressive historic buildings, UNESCO lists or famous events, its destinations extend to all kind of countries and cities - from Berlin and Barcelona to small villages along the Yantra river and the high planes of Peru. This geographical enlargement benefits communities that otherwise wouldn't have a shot in taking a piece of the profit in the cultural tourism.

The second big difference is exactly the profit distribution. While cultural tourism contributes to the local economy through tourism taxes, entrance fees to museums, events tickets, and souvenir buying (tourism and supporting industries exports), the creative tourism contribution goes beyond these benefits. First, in the cultural tourism, most of the tourism exports happen in the outbound market, where tour operators and travel agencies sell the product. Very few of the packaged tours profits or the individual traveler dollars go directly to the local community when it comes to international cultural tourism.

On the contrary, the creative tourism directly contributes to the local economy not only trough tourism exports, but through direct financial contribution to the local creative industries and the supporting local infrastructure.

Another issue with cultural tourism is the vast percentage of the so called "accidental cultural tourists" - travelers who use the product of the cultural tourism once at a destination, but their motivation to travel to this destination is not driven by its cultural assets. That makes financial projections, forecasts and planning very difficult, specially on the domestic markets. The research shows huge gaps in statistics about the so called "cultural tourist": only in the USA there is a difference between 78% (Mandala research) and 14% (NEA) on what percentage of all travelers are cultural heritage travelers.

Since creative tourism is driven by motivation to learn and participate in the creation of a cultural activity, it is much easier to distinguish the regular tourist from the creative one. That helps hugely all economic activities of forecasting, researching, and - ultimately -planning the creative tourism development.

While there are differences between cultural and creative tourism, the business model for creative tourism clearly shows that any destination of cultural tourism also can profit from creative tourism. This merger of different types of tourism finds very fertile ground through the creative tourism activities: creative and adventure tourism, cultural and creative tourism, archaeology tourism and creative tourism, wine & gourmet tourism and creative tourism, etc. Therefore, destinations that already have the assets to develop other type of tourism, as Barcelona, for example with its great resources for cultural tourism, are using this advantage for increasing their profit with creative tourism.

Additional advantages from creative tourism are the non-tangible benefits that it brings to communities. From identity building to attracting talent from other places, the creative industries flourish and contribute to the positive development of local communities. Once creative industries are developed because of creative tourism demand, the tangible benefits increase internally too through better business, real estate and overall human capital climate.

Creative Tourism New Zealand has been set up to promote a range of interactive workshops sampling the best New Zealand art and culture has to offer. Grown into a nationwide organization, CTNZ started in 2003 in the Nelson region with the help of the Nelson Bays Arts Marketing.

The workshop categories under which CTNZ promotes its tutors are reflective of traditional New Zealand values: Art, Maori Culture, Taste and Nature. The workshops are fun, informal and hands-on. The participants will enjoy spending time with the tutors, either at their homes or work places, while picking up a new skill and creating their own handcrafted souvenir. Many of the workshops are family friendly.

CONCEPT

Creative tourism has existed since tourism began, but has only recently been given its own name. Its originators are Greg Richards and Crispin Raymond, who have defined 'creative tourism' as "learning a skill on holiday that is part of the culture of the country or community being visited. Creative tourists develop their creative potential, and get closer to local people, through informal participation in interactive workshops and learning experiences that draw on the culture of their holiday destinations".

Values

We believe that Creative Tourism is a more sustainable form of tourism that can benefit the communities in which it is based, provide a new income source for tutors and inspire visitors. As tutors interact on a genuine and personal basis with workshop participants, a true cross-cultural understanding can take place.

Developments

The concept of 'creative tourism' is continuing to develop. In 2006, the "Creative Cities Network" endorsed by UNESCO, agreed on the following working definition of creative tourism: "Creative Tourism is travel directed towards an engaged and authentic experience, with participative learning in the arts, heritage, or special character of a place. It provides a connection with those who reside in this place and create this living culture." (See official website for more information: Creative Cities Network - UNESCO Culture Sector)

And more recently, the book: "Tourism, Creativity and Development" (2007) edited by Greg Richards and Julie Wilson "...] analyses the impact and effectiveness of creative strategies in tourism development and charts the emergence of 'creative tourism', ...] involving active participation by tourists in creative activities, skill development and/or creative challenges." Many tourists, they argue, now seem to want to become part of the local community and have direct contact with the everyday life of others. This lies at the very heart of what Creative Tourism New Zealand tries to promote.

In September 2008, the "Creative Cities Network" has been hosting a major conference on Creative Tourism to discuss and define creative tourism, showing examples of success and best practices. CTNZ has been invited to join the conference and presented the New Zealand experience to the conference (see

Official Website of Santa Fe Arts and Culture for more information). The main points studied in the conference are reported in a book called: "CREATIVE TOURISM, A GLOBAL CONVERSATION How to Provide Unique Creative Experiences for Travelers Worldwide". The book is available through Sunstone Press

Our vision for the future is to develop the concept of creative tourism as well as the network of workshops on offer while keeping true to our values of quality, authenticity, informality and fun.

If you are interested in joining us as a workshop Tutor click here for more info.

BLOGS AND GROUPS

A facebook group has been created to invite discussions about Creative Travel in New Zealand. If you are interested, please join the group: Creative Travel New Zealand on facebook or ask for an invitation to join by e-mailing: denise@creativetourism.co.nz.

Comments and ideas are also invited on this blog: Creative Tourism New Zealand: Explore New Zealand creatively!

THE PEOPLE

Crispin Raymond

Founder, Creative Tourism New Zealand

Originator, Creative Tourism concept.

Contact: crispin@creativetourism.co.nz

Crispin migrated to New Zealand in 2001 and lives in the Nelson-Tasman region, attracted by its mix of creative energy and natural beauty. Previously based in the UK, he worked in the arts for 25 years, firstly as Chief Executive of the Theatre Royal in Bath and subsequently as the founder of a specialist management consultancy to help arts and charitable organisations with policy, management, building and funding issues.

Greg Richards

Originator, Creative Tourism concept.

Contact: greg@tram-research.com

Greg is a physical geographer who moved into teaching tourism in the 1980s. While Director of the Centre for Leisure and Tourism Studies at the University of North London, he founded the Association for Tourism and Leisure Education (ATLAS) which initiated the EU funded European Cultural Tourism Survey in 1991. This research continues to develop new insights into the motivations and behaivour of visitors to cultural attractions. It was during discussions with Crispin at an ATLAS Winter University course in Portugal in 2000 that the emergence of the Creative Tourism phenomenon was first identified. Greg has written and edited many books and articles on cultural tourism and is leading the academic development of the creative tourism concept.

Denise Raymond

Manager, Creative Tourism New Zealand

Contact: denise@creativetourism.co.nz

Denise migrated to New Zealand with Crispin in 2001. Having chosen to live on a wonderful property in the hills near Motueka, most of their energy is spent on the land caring for the trees and propagating native plants. Denise has always been enthusiastic about the concept of creative tourism and has taken the role of manager in October 2005. Before that she had been working mainly as a translator and a French teacher.

Ali Boswijk

Chairman (non-executive), Creative Tourism New Zealand

Contact: boswijk@xtra.co.nz

During her previous role as CEO of Nelson Bays Arts Marketing, Ali was the first to recognise the potential for Creative Tourism in Nelson-Tasman and New Zealand. Ali brings with her extensive experience of both the local and national arts sector.

Sarah Moulder

Director, Creative Tourism New Zealand

Contact: sarah@coppermine.co.nz

Sarah's background is in the tourism and outdoor industries with experience as Australasian Marketing Manager of Kathmandu outdoor clothing company and Marketing Manager of the Youth Hostel Association of New Zealand. Sarah has recently moved to Nelson to enjoy the sunshine, outdoors and extensive range of creative experiences on offer in the region.

Claude Malet

Website Manager, Creative Tourism New Zealand

Contact: webmaster@creativetourism.co.nz

Computer Engineer and outdoors enthusiast. Used to spend summers tramping in the various South Island National and Forest Parks.

DRAFT TOURISM POLICY 2001 - 2010

DRAFT TOURISM POLICY 2001 - 2010

The purpose of this policy is to present a vision for tourism in Namibia in the next decade, its objectives and roles of stakeholders. Successful tourism requires that all key stakeholders work together: government, private sector and NGOs. This policy aims to provide the framework for that collaboration within strategies and programs to fit within it.

INTRODUCTION

The Namibian economy is dominated by the mining, fishing and agriculture sectors. As unemployment is high, Namibia needs to create increased employment opportunities. Tourism is a major user of people and offers significant opportunities for the employment of youth and has a gender bias towards women. Tourism has the lowest ratio of investment to job creation, many activities are immediately accessible to the previously disadvantaged part of the population. Tourism is a major source of foreign exchange (and via domestic tourism the retention of foreign exchange within the country). Tourism can provide funds for conservation of the country's fragile environment, has a substantial economic multiplier effect and generates tax revenues for Government.

The potential of Namibia's tourism sector is enormous. Namibia offers a range of unique and exciting natural, cultural and man-made resources that will, if planned and managed effectively, continue to attract increasing numbers of tourists. Namibia is committed to a sound conservation strategy, which will ensure that its attractions are not over-utilised and/or damaged. Namibia has good infrastructure and a strong private sector industry offering accommodation, transport and tours of good quantity and to a competitive standard. Namibia has established perceptions in its source markets of political stability, health and security, which relative to other African countries do not inhibit tourism.

An overall policy is required to make sure that tourism is developed in a sustainable, equitable and responsible manner to create a significant contribution to the economic development of Namibia and the quality of life of all her people.

Government, private sector, communities and stakeholder organisations (NGOs) are committed to working together to bring about the changes and improvements required to achieve this mission.

Policy Definition

Policy is a guide for making decisions in the future. Policy statements are made to indicate to those concerned just what the organisation will or will not do in pursuance of its overall purpose.

A good tourism policy provides definite and clear direction and at the same time allows for decision making within clearly stated limits.

The elements of the proposed tourism policy include:

- A profile of the existing industry and its performance.
- A tourism development philosophy.

- Social, economic and environmental objectives.
- A set of programs
- An institutional framework indicating roles for stakeholders

2. Profile Of The Existing Namibian Tourism Industry And Its Performance

Tourism in Namibia has a history of being developed around state owned resorts in protected areas. The product has been predominantly of a self-catering nature, mainly for national and regional (Southern African) travellers. Today, tourism is becoming an increasingly vital component of livelihood strategies for the communal and private farmers. Traditional farming activities are being complemented with tourism at so called guest farms and communal area residents are organising themselves in conservancies to create benefits from wildlife tourism.

There are indications that degradation of the environment, over-utilisation of scarce resources and the destruction or pollution of attractions is increasing throughout Namibia. Proper control of tourist activities is a prerequisite for responsible and sustainable tourism. It is therefore of prime importance that framework plans be prepared for the parks, communal conservancies and commercial land, which provide an enforceable guide for tourism activities in all these areas.

International arrival trends indicate a growth in multi-destination travel within Southern Africa by high-spending long-haul travellers. Such visitors like to combine highlights of the region into one itinerary. The tourism policy should take recognition of this fact and support the current number of important cross border parks being investigated by Namibia and her neighbours. These include initiatives with the Rightersveld in the Karas Region, as well similar projects in the Kunene and Caprivi Regions.

It must however, be recognised that the majority of Namibia's visitors are South Africans who travel overland and as they tend to make use of low yielding tourism facilities, currently add little in net value added terms to the tourism economy.

Little work if any, has been done in developing new or alternative source markets. The Namibia Tourism Board will have specific responsibilities in this area.

Nationally capacity utilisation is on average relatively low with bed occupancy rates averaging 36% in 1998. Service standards in most establishments and businesses serving the tourism industry are adequate. The quality of some of the smaller establishments, particularly in the communal areas, is variable. The importance of these small enterprises should however not be underestimated in terms of being the entry point of rural residents into the tourism industry. In an effort to maintain and improve overall standards programs of training have been initiated through the existing training establishments.

3. Objectives

Tourism development needs to be sustainable - economically, socially and environmentally. The Ministry has formulated various principles into a tourism development philosophy, which will guide the implementation of this overall strategy. The tourism policy will take due recognition of and strengthen the intent of existing policies and legislation (CBT Policy, Conservancy policy and legislation).

Philosophy

- The development and promotion of the tourism industry in Namibia will place emphasis on the country's natural, cultural and man-made resources.
- Tourism should be a legitimate land use, a vital industry and a critical development tool for the empowerment of previously disadvantaged groups as well as a means for diversification of livelihoods of communities on both private and communal land.
- Tourism development is equitable, with user-rights and responsibilities vested in 'host communities'
- The industry should develop in a manner, which will preserve the national pride and dignity of the peoples of Namibia, while

simultaneously encouraging visitors to experience their way of life.

- Tourism development requires a consultative planning process and subsequently the approved tourism plans must be implemented with monitoring by the relevant partners.
- In developing tourism products, infrastructure and related facilities, the Government will take into account the need to stimulate the expansion of domestic tourism within al layers of the population in harmony with the drive to increase international tourism arrivals.
- Ensure the international competitiveness of the Namibian tourism product through the development of a safe, reliable, quality product and encourage competitive marketing by all stakeholders.
- The Government will pursue a policy of exploiting the tourism market selectively; stressing to the various target groups the uniqueness of the tourism product within the destination.

The philosophy seeks to ensure that the industry evolves in a cohesive manner that permits the country to derive the greatest possible direct and indirect benefits from the investment of resources. These objectives are related to the division of sustainability -

Economic

The Tourism Policy seeks to ensure that the tourism industry makes a significant impact on the expansion of Namibia's economy by way of the following:

- The generation of substantial net foreign exchange earnings.
- The provision of direct employment opportunities at all levels within the industry.
- The provision of additional sources of income (profits, wages, rents, fees, etc.).
- The generation of linkages with other sectors of the economy e.g., agriculture, transport, handicraft, sports and construction.

- Consequential increase in the tax base.

Social

The Tourism Policy seeks to ensure that tourism serves as a vehicle for securing definite social gains to the population, in particular the previously disadvantaged while simultaneously avoiding and/or minimising as far as possible the negative aspects of tourism development activities. It aims to:

- Ensure that as far as possible all sections of the Namibian community benefit from tourism
- Encourage the development of those cultural forms and expressions, which are distinctly Namibian in origin, and development into new attractions.
- Promote greater international awareness of Namibia through the projection of Namibia's cultural forms.
- Foster greater national awareness and pride by attention to the preservation, restoration and promotion of historical sites, cultural festivals, art forms, natural scenic sites, etc.
- Protect historical and archaeological sites to ensure that the delicate balance of the physical environment is not threatened.
- Safeguard the physical and social territorial rights of residents especially with respect to the facilities where visitor numbers are likely to exceed the population of the established local community.
- Ensure the close cooperation and partnerships of key stakeholders at local, national and international levels.

Environmental

It should be acknowledged that tourism resources are found throughout the country in protected areas, on communal, on freehold land and in urban areas and that diversification of tourism is therefore required.

Namibia has a unique but fragile resource base and all stakeholders must strive to develop high quality low impact tourism products.

In order to protect the long-term future of the protected areas and their impact on their neighbour's livelihood, strategies must be developed to ensure that costs and benefits are shared equitably.

4. Programs and Policies

The policy identifies priority areas for support. These are based on a geographical and responsibility division and covers:

Protected Areas

The purpose of protected areas in Namibia includes the maintenance of relatively unspoiled areas for posterity and biodiversity improvement. These areas need to fulfill their potential in a responsible manner as engines of growth. The future of the protected areas relies on the integration within neighbouring economies. If done responsibly, improved management should also be a consequence of this approach.

Based on carefully planned exercises, protected areas should be utilised to an increased extent for the benefit of diversifying and complementing the tourism product of Namibia. National Parks and game reserve form the core attraction in Africa and in Namibia, there is scope to increase the international drawing power by increasing the utilisation of the protected areas in a sustainable manner.

Requirements:

- Implementation of the People and Parks Policy 1996.
- The clarification and enabling legislation re the rights of people living within parks.
- The establishment and implementation of tourism management plans which include integration of protected areas into surrounding economies.
- Standards, monitoring and evaluation of park products.
- Understanding of park management issues related to tourism utilisation.

Private Land

Private land has title deed that allows owners to exercise control over tourism. Private land has traditionally been utilised for agricultural purposes. Due to land degradation and enabling ministerial policies regarding wildlife since the 1970's, a booming consumptive and non-consumptive tourism industry has developed. Tourism development has however not been well planned and the impacts of tourism on the environment not always adequately addressed. Private land includes proclaimed towns and cities where much potential exists, but little "urban tourism" efforts have been initiated.

The enabling environment regarding tourism on private land is adequately addressed. This sector can function well in the free market within responsible tourism guidelines. Encouragement will be given to this sector to take a lead in innovative product development that can attract new market segments able to bring tangible benefits to Namibia. In that same context, there will be a discouragement for tourism initiatives that bring little or no benefits and have doubtful environmental impact like uncontrolled 4x4 routes.

Requirements

- Regional/National plans to be drawn up, standards set, monitoring systems of tourists data gathering and impacts of tourism on the environment to be introduced. Linkages with neighbouring land use types should be established. Identify training needs and introduce measures to address these needs.
- Local responsible tourism plans are to be done per proclaimed town or city to address local issues. This should include the promotion of diversification of activity e.g. cultural, craft, historic etc. issues such as improvement of the service industry should be addressed. The need for various establishments Bed and Breakfasts etc.
- Partners to develop, manage and market the tourism product.

The Communal Lands

Recognition for MET's communal conservancy policy has been obtained, nationally, regionally and internationally. This stems from the fact that conservancies enable rural dwellers to engage in the tourism market in a meaningful way as equal partners and direct benefits accrue to them in an equitable manner. Income from tourism is ploughed back into resource management and community development.

Communal lands have the potential to integrate tourism into all layers of Namibia's society. It can contribute effectively to the diversification of livelihood activities of rural communities which will add to the acceptance of the industry within Namibia.

Communal Conservancy legislation provides adequate rights and responsibilities for responsible consumptive utilisation of wildlife. Non-consumptive tourism is not addressed adequately to allow the effective management of tourism. This situation needs to be addressed and conservancies must be enabled to manage tourists and tourism effectively.

Requirements

- Implementation and strengthening of the Namibia Community-Based Tourism Policy.
- Implementation of the Communal Conservancy Legislation 1996.
- Strengthening of conservancy rights to manage tourism and tourists effectively on communal land.
- The introduction of incentives to investment and operation in the communal areas if their undertakings are certified as being sustainable.
- PTO application process formalised with due recognition of conservancies, Traditional Authorities, Regional Council, MLRR and MET.
- Investor security through legally binding contracts with conservancies.

In addition to the policy for these geographical areas, there are programs required related to:

Marketing

Although at present there are numerous activities offered such as ballooning, horse riding, camel trails, hunting, angling, hiking, bird watching, photography, camping, yachting, cruises, star - gazing and adventure tourism (skydiving and paragliding, dune adventures, rock climbing, gliding, caving, mountain biking, white water rafting), the main volume in terms of revenue and visitor numbers is still found in general purpose tours, either guided or on a self drive basis.

A strategy of precision targeting will be pursued for maximum effectiveness. Accordingly, marketing initiatives will stress the following:

- Tourism development in Namibia will not be based on mass tourism but in finding and exploiting specialist niche markets.
- The international tourism promotion effort will be aimed at a low volume, high yield customers.
- The fostering of support amongst the travel trade in the source markets, including carriers as well as the establishment of joint marketing programs wherever possible.
- Improving the information infrastructure to facilitate easier access by potential customers to information, reservation services, etc.
- The availability of tourism products and facilities for the domestic market.

Continuous research both amongst arriving/departing visitors as well as in the source markets will be carried out in order that trends can be identified, basic data assembled and that performance of the sector can be monitored

In order to achieve the anticipated growth of the industry and the success of a marketing drive a programme to ensure product readiness and acceptability will be undertaken as an essential part of the strategy. Attention will be focused on upgrading all tourism facilities.

It is recognised that the following are basic prerequisites for sustaining the appeal of the destination to the above average income visitor who faces so many competing choices -

- Accommodation, which is simple, clean, functional and in harmony with the environment and which meets the minimum requirements as set out in the regulations.
- Service in tourism facilities which is warm, friendly, sincere and efficient.
- Food which is wholesome, fresh, hygienically stored and served,
- Tourism facilities which are accessible, convenient, and which reflect a high degree of efficiency, maintenance and management.

The lead role in marketing will be played by the Namibia Tourism Board.

Investment Incentives

The Government of Namibia is committed to the supply of appropriate improvements in infrastructure and plans to rely on private capital to spearhead the expansion of tourism. In so doing, Government will welcome appropriate investment by both foreign and domestic capital.

Preference will be given to those investors who can demonstrate credibility and successful experience with respect to the operation of such facilities and who offer sound prospects for tapping targeted niches within source markets.

Selective use will be made of financial incentives in order to obtain the type, quality and quantity of tourism facilities required by the market place. Such facilities may also apply to repair, renewal, refurbishing and extension of existing facilities.

5. Institutional Framework

The Role of Government

Tourism within Namibia comes under the auspices of the Ministry of Environment and Tourism, which has a Directorate of Tourism responsible for the development of policy and the gathering and dissemination of tourism statistics.

Government's main role will be in the creation of an enabling environment for responsible private sector tourism to operate throughout Namibia. This will mean that:

- Responsible tourism implementation will be monitored by Government
- The creation of tourism investment incentives will be introduced.
- The implementation and enforcement of regional and local tourism plans, integrating consumptive and non - consumptive tourism into existing land use practises where appropriate
- Development, promotion and support of craft, historical, artistic and cultural, in addition to existing traditional attractions of Namibia.
- Discouragement of products without tangible benefits (e.g. 4x4 routes).
- Proclamation of national monuments without limiting responsible tourism access to these sites and applying for the listing of World Heritage sites with the United Nations
- Adaptive management using 'Limits of acceptable change' will be investigated.
- Dialogue with other Ministries in issues related to sustainable tourism development.

The Regional Tourism Organisation of Southern Africa, RETOSA, was formed in 1996 to act as the tourism marketing arm of SADC and promote the tourist attractions and services of the region to source markets. During 1998, a Tourism Protocol for the SADC region was also ratified which has as its aim the facilitation of tourism to and within the region. Namibia is a full member of WTO.

Affiliated government tourism institutions include:

Namibia Tourism Board

The Namibia Tourism Board in conjunction with the private sector and the ministry, will be responsible for marketing of the tourism product including:

- Actively market and promote Namibia as the premier tourism destination
- Actively promote successes in the communal areas locally, nationally and internationally.
- Use the local and international media to recognise and promote establishments that take action to become socially and environmentally responsible
- Encourage successful responsible tourism suppliers to champion the cause of the communities and the spread of Responsible Tourism

Human resource development & training will be a key responsibility of the NTB.

There is a need to establish a standard national qualification framework for the tourism sector. All levels of training should be considered for accreditation including community level.

The NTB will also be responsible for the creation of industry standards.

Namibia Wildlife Resorts

As operators of tourism accommodation within Namibia's protected areas, Namibia Wildlife Resorts play a key role in the development of tourism. It is recognised that the facilities are inherited from a pre-independence period and that the product needs to be adapted to fit market demand, as well as overall development objectives of the country.

Air Namibia

As the national carrier responsible for the majority of air transport facilities, domestically, regionally and internationally, the airline plays a pivital role in the supply of customers to Namibia's diverse tourism products. A close working relationship between the NTB, the industry and Air Namibia will be important. Jointly funded marketing programs will be encouraged.

The Role of the Private Sector

The private tourism sector in Namibia is represented by the Federation of Namibia Tourist Associations (FENATA) of which the following tourism organisations are members:

- Hospitality Association of Namibia (HAN)
- Tour & Safari Association of Namibia (TASA)
- Car Rental Association of Namibia (CARAN)
- Tourism-related Namibian Business Association (TRENABA)
- Namibia Community-based Tourism Association (NACOBTA)
- Namibia Professional Hunters' Association (NAPHA)
- Association of Namibian Travel Agents (ANTA)

Other private sector associations are: -

- Regional and Publicity Associations, e.g. Namib i, Etosha i and Southern Tourism Forum
- Conservancy associations (CANAN)

The private sector is the operator of tourism in Namibia. It is recognised that they have created trust with the industry in the various source markets which is beneficial for the whole country. These relations need to be kept and expanded.

Although the product offered by the industry has been successful in the markets it was targeted for, the industry is encouraged to expand their product to different markets and to take recognition of broad development issues to which the tourism industry can contribute. These are mainly related to integrating previously disadvantaged groups into the industry as players and recipients of tourism benefits.

The industry is encouraged to enter into partnerships with community organisations to develop tourism in a responsible manner. Their contributions may include:

- Capital investment
- Management expertise
- Transfer skills to communal area provision of capital investments
- Assistance in marketing and other technical areas.

The Role of NGOs

NGOs, particularly those with an environmental and community-based focus, are expected to play a vital role in the development and spread of responsible tourism practices. They are expected to play the following roles:

- Contribute to the development of policies and plans for the tourism industry
- Assist government in developing standards for responsible tourism
- Assist government, private sector and communities in implementing, monitoring and evaluating responsible tourism
- Source funding from donor agencies to develop specific community-based tourism projects
- Assist communities and community groups in getting organised, preparing themselves for tourism and implementing tourism projects
- Assist government in conducting tourism and environmental awareness programs among communities and the tourism industry at large
- Liase between the private sector and communities to generate more community involvement in the tourism sector and stronger private sector commitment
- Deliver education, training and bridging courses to local communities

MET/ NGO partnerships include:

- Namibian Association for Community Based Natural Resource Management Support Organisations (NACSO)

The Role of Communities

Communities should ideally be seen as private sector players in the tourism industry. However, it is recognised that their entry is of a disadvantaged position and that additional effort by all other stakeholders need to be made to achieve the overall objectives through tourism development.

Communities should be involved in the development of tourism in the following ways:

- Organise themselves at all levels (national, provincial and local) to play a more effective role in the tourism industry and interact with government and role players at all levels
- Oppose developments that are harmful to the local environment and culture of the community
- Conservancy development
- Raising community awareness of resource management and tourism.
- Commitment to developing tourism related enterprises to contribute to economic development of local community.
- Maintain and develop traditions and encourage cultural tourism
- Enter into joint venture partnerships with private sector
- The provision of a conducive tourism environment.
- Actively participate in and promote responsible tourism

Chapter 4

ARTS, CRAFTS AND TOURISM

Bhutan has a rich and unique cultural heritage that has largely remained intact because of its isolation from the rest of the world until the early 1960s. One of the main attractions for tourists is the country's culture and traditions. Bhutanese tradition is deeply steeped in its Buddhist heritage. Hinduism is the second dominant religion in Bhutan, being most prevalent in the southern regions. Both religions co-exist peacefully and receive support from the government, and enjoy royal patronage. The government is increasingly making efforts to preserve and sustain the current culture and traditions of the country. Because of its largely unspoiled natural environment and cultural heritage, Bhutan has been referred to as The Last Shangri-la.

While Bhutanese citizens are free to travel abroad, Bhutan is viewed as inaccessible by many foreigners. There is a widespread misconception that Bhutan has set limits on tourist visas. Another reason for it being an unpopular destination is the cost, which is high for tourists on tighter budgets. Entry is free for citizens of India and Bangladesh, but all other foreigners are required to sign up with a Bhutanese tour operator and pay around $200 per day that they stay in the country.

The National Dress for Bhutanese men is the gho, a knee-length robe tied at the waist by a cloth belt known as the kera.

Women wear an ankle-length dress, the kira, which is clipped at one shoulder and tied at the waist. An accompaniment to the kira is a long-sleeved blouse, the toego, which is worn underneath the outer layer. Social status and class determine the texture, colours, and decorations that embellish the garments. Differently coloured scarves and shawls are important indicators of social standing, as Bhutan has traditionally been a feudal society. Jewellery is mostly worn by women, especially during religious festivals and public gatherings. To strengthen Bhutan's identity as an independent country, Bhutanese law requires all Bhutanese citizens to wear the national dress in public areas and as formal wear.

Rice, buckwheat, and increasingly maize, are the staple foods of the country. The local diet also includes pork, beef, yak meat, chicken, and mutton. Soups and stews of meat and dried vegetables spiced with chillies and cheese are prepared. Ema datshi, made very spicy with cheese and chilies, might be called the national dish for its ubiquity and the pride that Bhutanese have for it. Dairy foods, particularly butter and cheese from yaks and cows, are also popular, and indeed almost all milk is turned to butter and cheese. Popular beverages include butter tea, tea, locally brewed rice wine and beer. Bhutan is the only country in the world to have banned the sale of tobacco.

Changlimithang Stadium, during a parade.

Chaam, sacred masked dances, are annually performed during religious festivals.

Bhutan's national sport is archery, and competitions are held regularly in most villages. It differs from Olympic standards in technical details such as the placement of the targets and atmosphere. There are two targets placed over 100 meters apart and teams shoot from one end of the field to the other. Each member of the team shoots two arrows per round. Traditional Bhutanese archery is a social event and competitions are organized between villages, towns, and amateur teams. There are usually plenty of food and drink complete with singing and dancing. Attempts to distract an opponent include standing around the target and making fun of the shooter's ability. Darts (khuru) is an equally popular outdoor team sport, in which heavy wooden darts pointed with a 10 cm nail are thrown at a paperback-sized target ten to 20 meters away.

Another traditional sport is the digor, which resembles the shot put and horseshoe throwing. Cricket has gained popularity in Bhutan, particularly since the introduction of television channels from India. The Bhutan national cricket team is one of the more successful affiliate nations in the region. Football is also an increasingly popular sport. In 2002, Bhutan's national football (soccer) team played Montserrat, in what was billed as The Other Final; the match took place on the same day Brazil played Germany in the World Cup final, but at the time Bhutan and Montserrat were the world's two lowest ranked teams. The match was held in Thimphu's Changlimithang National Stadium, and Bhutan won 4-0. A documentary of the match was made by the Dutch filmmaker Johan Kramer.

Rigsar is an emerging style of popular music in Bhutan, played on a mix of traditional instruments and electronic keyboards, and dates back to the early 1990s; it shows the influence of Indian popular music, a hybrid form of traditional and Western popular influences. Traditional genres include the zhungdra and boedra.

Characteristic of the region is a type of castle fortress known as the dzong. Since ancient times, the dzongs have served as the religious and secular administration centres for their respective districts.

Bhutan has numerous public holidays, most of which centre around traditional seasonal, secular and religious festivals. They include the winter solstice (around January 1, depending on the lunar calendar), the lunar New Year (February or March), the King's birthday and the anniversary of his coronation, the official start of monsoon season (September 22), National Day (December 17), and various Buddhist and Hindu celebrations.

Masked dances and dance dramas are common traditional features at festivals, usually accompanied by traditional music.

Energetic dancers, wearing colourful wooden or composition face masks and stylized costumes, depict heroes, demons, dæmons, death heads, animals, gods, and caricatures of common people. The dancers enjoy royal patronage, and preserve ancient folk and religious customs and perpetuate the ancient lore and art of mask-making.

Inheritance in Bhutan generally goes in the female rather than the male line. Daughters will inherit their parents' house. A man is expected to make his own way in the world and often moves to his wife's home. Love marriages are common in urban areas, but the tradition of arranged marriages is still common in the villages. Although uncommon, polygamy is accepted, often being a device to keep property in a contained family unit rather than dispersing it. The previous King Jigme Singye Wangchuck, who abdicated in 2006, has 4 Queens, all of whom are sisters.

Arts & Crafts

Bhutan's arts and crafts reflect the unique spirit and identity of the Himalayan kingdom.

The art of Zorig Chosum - or the thirteen arts and crafts of Bhutan - remains very much alive today. They include carpentry, blacksmithing, weaving, sculpting and many of the crafts described below. There are two institutes of Zorig Chosum where these traditional arts and crafts are being taught today - one in the capital, Thimphu, and the other in Trashi Yangtse in eastern Bhutan.

The arts and crafts continue to thrive despite a small tourist market. Much of this is due to the government's support and emphasis on the preservation of culture and tradition.

Textiles

Bhutan's textiles are an integral part of daily life in this Himalayan kingdom. Gifts of cloth are offered at birth and death, and during auspicious occasions, weddings, and when someone gets promoted to higher level in his/her profession. Textiles are fashioned into clothing, crafts, and various kinds of containers.

Bhutanese textiles are renowned for their distinctive patterns inspired by nature. Each region has a specialised design. Bumthang, for example, is known for its vegetable dyed wool weaves called yathra, and exquisite pure silk weavings, Kishuthara, are famous in the eastern region of Lhuentse where it originates.

Weavers, mostly women in remote communities, pride themselves on being able to create textiles that reflect a visually stunning combination of colour, texture, pattern and composition. Bhutan is holding on to this traditional skill despite rapid modernisation.

Bhutanese textiles are now prized among collectors as a rare art-form that is being practiced only among a very small community in the remote Kingdom of Bhutan.

Paintings

Most Bhutanese art, including painting, are religious by nature. And because it is the process of creating the paintings that is important, most traditional painting is anonymous without an artist's signature.

The Bhutanese tradition of painting is called lhazo. This refers to all types of painting including traditional paintings, called thangkhas, which are scroll paintings of Buddhist iconography executed in mineral paints.

Bhutanese paintings of religious and other symbolic motifs also adorn houses in Bhutan, both inside the home and on exterior walls.

Thangkha style painting is highly stylised and strict geometric proportions are followed.

Sculptures

Bhutanese sculptors are well known in the Himalayan region. Many famous sculptors have been, and still are, making clay statues of Buddhist figures for important monasteries in the region.

Clay is the traditional material for local sculpture, known as jinzob. The art is expressed in statues and ritual objects and can be seen in the numerous monasteries throughout Bhutan. Many of Bhutan's monasteries boast of exceedingly fine central statues that sometimes rise up as high as three floors.

The art of sculpture is being kept alive at the Institute of Zorig Chosum where it is taught as a core subject.

Paper Making

The Bhutanese have always used their own handmade paper called deysho. Made of the bark of the daphne plant, this paper is used for the printing of religious texts, traditional books as well as for wrapping gifts. It is an extremely durable paper that is fairly resistant to insects.

Traditional paper making continues as an additional activity on the farm to earn some extra income for the paper makers.

A few paper factories have been established and some of them are now producing ornamental art paper with the inclusion of flower petals, and leaves, and other materials. Vegetable dyed paper is also being made for special occasions.

Wood Carving

The carving of wood is an ancient craft that continues to play an important role in modern Bhutan. The numerous prayer flags that flutter across the vast ridges of Bhutan are all printed from carved wooden blocks.

Parzo, or the craft of carving is not restricted only to wood. Carving is also done on slate and stone. Woodcarving is, however, the most common. It is used for making wooden blocks to print traditional books that are still much highly sought after today.

The wood is usually collected and seasoned for more than a year before it is carved. Bhutan's artisans are also well known for their highly skilled wooden carvings which adorn pillars and windows in monasteries, offices and public buildings.

Sword Making

The art of sword making falls under the tradition of garzo (or blacksmithing) which includes the making of all metal implements including knives, chains, darts etc.

Today, ceremonial swords are now a highly specialised craft. They are still being made for the gentry or senior officials who have been ceremoniously honoured. Ceremonial swords are worn on all special occasions while almost every Bhutanese male, even children, wear a traditional short knife called the dudzom.

History has it that Bhutan's best known sword maker was the treasure discoverer, Terton Pema Lingpa, from central Bhutan.

Boot Making

For ceremonial occasions, it is not uncommon to see Bhutanese men wear traditional boots made of cloth that is handstitched, embroided and appliquéd in Bhutanese motifs. The different colours used on the boot signify the rank and status of the person; hence, Ministers wear orange, senior officials wear red and the laity wears white.

There has been a revival of traditional boot making in recent years. Popularised by the emphasis on preservation of culture and tradition, boot making is also a subject taught at the Institute of Zorig Chosum. There are also shorter boots that reach above the ankle for women. Traditional Bhutanese boots are a must for formal events, and lend a ceremonial air to such occasions. Many villagers and retired monks also wear simpler traditional boots without the fancy appliqué work.

Bamboo Craft

The art of working with cane and bamboo is called thazo. Certain regions in Bhutan are famed for its bamboo and cane craft.

Rural communities in Zhemgang and Trongsa produce a variety of crafts with these materials. They include the distinctive bamboo hat called the belo that is still popular with the people in the area, and the still popular Bhutanese "Tupperware" basket called the bangchung.

The popular folk craft also include baskets of varying sizes for the home and for travel on horseback, and containers for carrying local drinks , the homebrew called arra.

Bow and Arrow Making

With archery as a national sport, the making of bamboo bows and arrows are picking up momentum once again particularly just before the annual national archery competition.

Many of the craftsmen look out for specific types of bamboo and mountain reeds to be fashioned into bows and arrows. These are picked at particular seasons, whittled down to size and expertly fashioned into the bow and arrow that has enabled Bhutanese men and youth to play a unique form of archery over the centuries. A well made set of bows and arrows are instrumental to a good game of archery.

Jewelry

Traditional Bhutanese jewelry is usually silver and gold jewelry with intricate motifs. They include heavy bracelets, komas or fasteners for the traditional women's dress, the kira, loop ear rings set with turquoise, and necklaces of the most valued stones in the Himalayan region - antique turquoise, coral beads and the zhi stone.

The zhi stone is a highly prized stone in Bhutan and among Himalayan Buddhists who believe in its protective powers. The stone is distinguished by its black and white spiral designs called "eyes". The zhi is believed to be an agate which were made into the zhi bead. There are now many replicas of the ancient zhi stone available in the market.

The best place to see Bhutanese jewelry is during a local festival where women turn up in their finery and jewelry. Some of them are draped with the traditional necklaces of coral, the size of small stones.

CHAPTER 5

PUBLICITY AND MARKET POTENTIAL OF CREATIVE TOURISM

The ultimate form of cultural tourism - experiencing the creation of cultural values in the creative tourism - continues to be a big trend in destination marketing. The focus is on local arts, crafts, gastronomy, wine culture, and everything that a place can offer. Combined with the brand war between similar places to show their uniqueness, the main element of the tourism product for creative tourism is the local focus.

Is this the right approach? Yes and no.

THE DESTINATION APPROACH

The traveler interested in creative tourism will be appealed by the right destination promotion that offers a lot of possibilities for creative travel. They will choose a destination because of its overall appeal and the possibility to participate in the exiting experiences of creative tourism. In this sense, the destination approach should be focused on the local ambiance and uniqueness of this destination or city. That is true for 61% for the US cultural traveler and 28% of the European cultural traveler. On both side of the Atlantic the first most important reason to choose a destination is its overall appeal - its cultural environment. But it this enough?

The Passion Approach

From all cultural travelers in the USA, 23 % started with a certain type of travel experience in mind when planning their next trip. In Europe, from those whose main choice for travel was to experience culture, 38% cited the cultural heritage as main reason to choose a destination. This is in actuality the market for cultural and creative tourism: the main motivation behind the travel is to experience culture, not only to participate in cultural activities while traveling to a destination. In other words, this is the choice of the concrete passion of the individual: it is more important to make a tour of the Roman Empire heritage or the Frank Lloyd Write architecture, than to visit Italy or Chicago per se.

Understanding this trend, UNESCO created the Creative Cities Network. Music lovers have choices from Italy to Spain, folk arts and crafts enthusiasts will be delighted to travel from Santa Fe to Aswan, Egypt. And while the gold seal of the UNESCO prestige worldwide provides these chosen destinations with enormous potential for marketing based on the UNESCO name only, other destinations should consider much more proactive measures in order to appeal to the cultural traveler, who pursue a passion.

Niche Marketing Vital For Creative Tourism Destinations

Destinations tend to focus on marketing the overall product in order to appeal to larger groups of travelers. For big cities or clusters of monotypes of attractions (business, meetings, etc.) this works perfectly. Take for example Hamburg: the world city for industrial trade shows. No matter that Hamburg has a lot to offer to cultural travelers, the city is positioning itself as the number one MICE city in Europe and with brilliant success. Munich, on the other side, another MICE and super economic power city, have chosen the Oktoberfest, the most famous beer festival in the world, to attract tourism.

Are DMOs taking in account what niche they can appeal and deliver this message to the passionate travelers searching creative tourism experiences? Not always. They tend to present the uniqueness of a destination through a complex mix of "everything for everyone". Event promotion for unique events, such as the Rose Festival in the Valley of the Thracian Kings, Bulgaria, Vienna New Year Concert or Milan Scala opera performances, is a very good approach, but is time limited to the duration of the event.

That is why destinations have to choose a typical characteristic, a mono-interest group of attractions appealing to one passion, one aspect of the city or micro-region/cluster to promote themselves to the cultural traveler. This positioning should fill the gap in the sentence: Our (destination, city, place) is the only one in the world where you can .... (learn how to bind your books with leather, paint on brown ceramics, craft your own cloisonné, etc.).

Peru, as a country, position itself as the only place to learn how to wave their incredible Inca style fabrics, and if you want to learn how to do it, this is the place to go. Chile, on the other side, where the same carpet weaving has the exactly same traditions, does not focus on Inca carpet weaving. Santa Fe is the destination par excellence for crafts related with earth-ware and American folk arts, and is the biggest success for creative tourism in North America.

Destinations (from countries to small cities), should explore the possibility to brand, position and market themselves focused on these passions, without, of course, abandoning the overall appeal of the place, appealing to mass tourism. How they can do that?

Create

Determine which group of attractions, activities and infrastructure has the most unique potential to develop creative tourism product. For more information how to become a creative tourism destination, check up these articles. Increase market geography by choosing an uniquely global product. If your city, micro-region is too small, extend the region until finding the right unique product. Example: create a cultural landscape of all wine routes in your state (like Virginia is doing it) and package it together under one product: "Virginia wine making". For certain interests, you will need bigger territory and several destinations under the same product (American Arts and Crafts Movement), for some destinations you will need only one product, like tile painting in Ybor, Florida.

Brand, position, promote and globalize: Create a group of tourism products (programs, projects, developments in the urban structure or the geographic micro-region) and brand it as "The only place where..."

Promote it globally to the niche markets. Maybe in Germany there are not enough potential travelers to go to Iowa City (UNESCO creative city for literature) to learn modern American literature, but for sure worldwide there are enough Kurt Vonnegut enthusiasts who will travel to the "Athens of the Midwest" to create a stable tourism income.

No matter what approach takes a DMO - a geographic or a specialization one, the most important is to show globally that this destination is THE place to create, experience and enjoy creative travel now, only here and to a very specific narrow niche demanding traveler. And, there is an enormous opportunity for DMOs and travel organizations (travel agencies, hotel owners, etc.) to capitalize on any of thee above approaches to destination marketing for creative tourism. In the USA, there is a gap of 67% between the desire to participate in creative activities (Mandala Research) and the real participation. Countries in emerging destinations, such as Chile, Vietnam, Cuba, Jordan, Egypt, Morocco, and all Balkan countries, have unique treasures to offer and shape their destinations in an innovative way to serve the creative tourism. That combined with the fact that they are still in the list "to discover" gives them unique edge to promote creative tourism since the very beginning of destination development - a change to not miss now.

Research based on Mandala Research Report "The American Cultural Tourist" and the European Traveler Profile Report (download .pdf).

Creative tourism: 5 important considerations for developing creative tourism destinations:

Part One: Intro

Part Two: Location

Part Three: Human Capital and Attitude

Part Four: Target Markets, Strategies, Sustainability, Financing

Part Five: Advertising, Promotion and Authenticity

'Tourism that offers visitors a creative pursuit (including arts, crafts and cookery workshops), with the opportunity to stay in high quality accommodation, and to connect with local people in a distinctive destination.'

Recent research from the Henley Centre shows that people want more time, space and energy, and a greater sense of wellbeing. They are demonstrating a growing desire to connect with each other and feel more in touch with local communities. Some of this can be achieved through creative tourism as it provides visitors with the opportunity to learn a new skill, provide a sense of achievement and to create a unique souvenir, for example, a painting, crafted object or food product. This type of break is also more likely to give people a lasting emotional attachment to the destination and will encourage them to recommend and also revisit the destination.

Even with the current downturn in the economy many people still feel that a holiday is fundamental and a destination that offers the opportunity to learn something at the same time as providing a change of scene will gain a competitive edge.

If you are interested in developing workshops for the visitor market we would also love to hear from you and am particularly interested in;

" Visual artists for watercolour, pastel and oil painting

" Sculptors

" Potters

" Metalworkers

" Jewellers

" Furniture makers

" Glassmakers

" Wood carvers

" Craftspeople for knitting, textiles, weaving, embroidery

" Traditional Kentish crafts e.g. beer making, decorating with hops

" Chefs cooking with local Kent produce, e.g. oysters, mussels, fish, food foraged in the Kent countryside

" Food producers for cheese making, cooking with apples etc.

" Vineyards for winemaking, farms/orchards for cider, apple juice

Be more innovative and creative, tourism players told

MUAR: Players in the tourism industry have been urged to be more innovative and creative in exploiting and capitalising on products that are unique to their areas.

Tourism Minister Datuk Seri Dr Ng Yen Yen said every product, no matter how small, had the potential to attract visitors and tourists.

She said the players, including the relevant departments, should also know how to promote and sell the products in an attractive package.

"Take Muar, for example, which has a beautiful river, beautiful old buildings as well as old trees which add beauty to the town's scenery.

"The river, the buildings and the trees have a certain heritage and we can promote them in our tourism packages," she said yesterday.

Dr Ng said the town was also popular for its food such as satay, mee bandung and asam pedas and players could promote Muar as a food destination. She said Muar was also the only district in the country which had a Barongan dance group.

She said the group, from Kampung Parit Bugis in Sungai Balang, could be engaged to perform at Tanjung Emas near the estuary during weekends.

Dr Ng said these initiatives would add value to the tourism industry.

Creative tourism is a form of cultural tourism and has been described as 'Tourism which offers visitors the opportunity to develop their creative potential through active participation in courses and learning experiences, which are characteristic of the holiday destination where they are taken.'

A further definition, used by Catriona Campbell to describe her creative tourism business is:

'Tourism that offers visitors a creative pursuit (including arts, crafts and cookery workshops), with the opportunity to stay in high quality accommodation, and to connect with local people in a distinctive destination.'

Cultural tourism, on the other hand, is described by Susan Briggs as follows.

'Tourism motivated wholly, or in part by interest in the historical, artistic or lifestyle/heritage offerings of a tourism destination' and emerged to meet the demand from visitors looking for more than 'sun, sea and sand' mass market experiences. It encourages arts and tourism sectors to work more closely together and it encompasses visits to enjoy visual and performing arts, museums, galleries, heritage attractions, artists open studios, art fairs, auctions, public art and architecture, films, festivals and other cultural events.'

The difference between cultural and creative tourism is that creative tourists participate in a creative activity when visiting a destination whilst cultural tourists are consumers of cultural experiences.

Why Creative Tourism?

Creative tourism is not new, people have been engaging in creative educational and learning experiences on holiday for a long time, but it is growing in popularity. More people are looking for authentic experiences and want to engage with local communities as well as, or instead of, being passive consumers of cultural experiences provided in the destination.

Connection and Authentic Experiences

Research sponsored by Enjoy England shows that people want more time, space and energy, and a greater sense of wellbeing and are demonstrating a growing desire to connect with each other and feel more in touch with local communities. A creative tourism break can provide this and also provide people with a sense of achievement through learning a new skill. Also, by creating their own souvenir, whether a painting, crafted object, poem or even a recipe, people are more likely to have a lasting emotional attachment for the creative tourism destination, to talk, blog or tweet about in a positive way and to return again.

The roots of creative tourism, as we now understand it, probably go back to the mid-1990s when the European Commission funded the Eurotex project to help craft producers in Portugal who needed to distinguish their handmade goods from those that were mass produced. It was realised that unless people understood what work went into making these goods they would not pay a realistic price for them. As a result the Alto Minho craft trail was developed that allowed visitors to meet the crafters, watch them at work and participate in the making of textiles .

Since then many destinations around the world have been considering and developing their own versions of creative tourism products, partly in recognition that people want participatory experiences but also because they are looking for new ways to interact with their visitors to provide differentiation from competing destinations.

Cultural tourism has been seen by many destinations as the antidote for low quality mass tourism but many visitors are now becoming disillusioned by traditional cultural mass market experiences. At the Santa Fe Creative Tourism Conference in 2008, Greg Richards stated :

'Trooping through cathedrals or museums or art galleries with hundreds of other people is increasingly being seen as an experience to be avoided rather than desired.'

Many visitors prefer to seek out small scale, out of the way places that other cultural tourists have not yet found. What the tourist is seeking in these local places is to experience the destination as the local would, to feel part of the community and to enjoy more contact with real people and engagement with local culture.

Developing Creative Potential

Creative tourism allows visitors to get even closer to local people through participation in interactive workshops and informal learning experiences that draw on the culture of their holiday destinations and, at the same time, develop their creative potential.

Creative tourism experiences offered around the world are diverse:

" bone carving with Maori tutors delivered through Creative New Zealand

" gastronomic breaks in Barcelona where participants learn about and shop for produce in La Boquera, the outdoor market, before being taught how to cook them

" Native American pottery workshops in Santa Fe to Ceòlas

" a music and dance summer school in South Uist, Scotland, featuring tuition in piping, fiddling, singing, dancing and the Gaelic language.

Is There a Market for Creative Tourism?

There is a huge growth in interest in undertaking craft activities and a significant number of people interested in participating in the arts. Department for Culture Media and Sport (DCMS) research indicated that 17% of the population took part in a craft activity in 2008/9 .

The 'Make Do and Mend' movement, last seen in the UK in the 40s, is also being revived, in part due to the recession but also because of (particularly young people's) concern for the planet.

People want to learn skills no longer taught in schools in interesting fun venues (not a description that could be applied to most adult education centres) and businesses are beginning to respond to this demand. The success of The Make Lounge in Islington, London that offers; 'Contemporary craft workshops with a stylish, social twist - perfect for embracing the 'make do and mend' ethic in a fashionable way' has encouraged others to provide similar offerings in a variety of locations. These include Craft Guerilla in East London, Craft Mafia which has chapters in Nottingham, Manchester and Glasgow and COW at The Custard Factory in Birmingham.

Amongst the top 20 worldwide trends forecast for 2010 is that the 'Make It Yourself' movement will become culturally acceptable across all social groups as people become nostalgic for past times and conspicuous consumption continues to be seen as unacceptable in difficult economic times. The popularity of Kirsty's Homemade Home on Channel 4 in 2009 is another example of this.

A Short Break with a Difference

The recession is also encouraging more people to want to 'escape' from their routines even if only for a short time and to desire a small treat occasionally. A short break away from home that also offers the opportunity to learn a new skill will fulfil this desire and will become increasingly popular.

Destinations and operators should look to their existing short break cultural tourism market profiles to find segments within that will respond to a creative tourism message. In addition they should look at creative professionals who are known to want to undertake creative activities outside of the workplace to enhance their existing artistic practice or as part of continuing professional development.

Domestic and Overseas Visitor Appeal

There is definitely a market for creative tourism amongst domestic visitors, including those concerned with reducing their carbon footprint, those who are cash rich and time poor (and unable to commit to long courses) and people wishing to take up a creative pursuit or revisit one they have not undertaken since leaving school.

There also appears to be a groups market, particularly female groups, for hen parties and 'girly' weekends for example. Creative pursuits are also likely to appeal to single travellers of all nationalities who know that they will share a common interest with the people they meet on a break.

In addition to providing differentiation and an added dimension to existing cultural experiences, creative tourism provides destinations and operators with good opportunities to extend their season as it is not usually weather dependent.

For overseas markets, visitors who respond to cultural tourism messages are also likely to be interested in the added dimension that creative tourism offers, particularly the opportunity to meet local people in distinctive settings. Venues like castles, stately homes and other attractions should all consider whether they can add the opportunity to engage in a creative pursuit to enhance the visitor experience.

The Market Profile

Research undertaken amongst participants of two pilot creative tourism events in 2009 showed that participants were predominantly female, aged 45 plus and likely to have children who are teenagers or who have now left home. The other large group was younger women aged between 22 and 30 with busy full-time jobs and no children. The participants also included creative professionals looking to add to their artistic practice and teachers wishing to 'be on the other side for a change!'

This research echoes the findings of segmentation research undertaken by the Art Council into the English population's engagement with the arts. This research identified thirteen arts consumer segments, including those most interested in participating in the arts. Two of the groups identified were:

" Urban arts eclectic (5% of English adults)

Highly qualified, young - half under 35, with no children, living in urban areas, affluent, and in the early stages of their career. One sixth from black and minority ethnic backgrounds. This segment contains the most active arts participants with interests ranging from dance, computer art, photography, music and creative writing.

" Traditional culture vultures (4% of English adults)

Majority are women, two thirds aged 45 to 74, living with a partner without any children, highly educated, high proportion (25%) living in rural areas and their interest in the arts extends into their participation in textile arts, photography, playing musical instruments, painting and drawing.

It is possible to conclude that those people already interested in and actively engaging in the arts and culture will also be motivated by creative tourism opportunities.

Beautiful, unusual and distinctive venues will inspire all sorts of creativity, including painting, photography, sculpture and creative writing. The opportunity to cook with local ingredients is also motivating. As previously mentioned, Barcelona offers gastronomy breaks and, in the UK, Padstow is renowned not only for its fish restaurants run by Rick Stein but also for the cookery courses his business provides at the Padstow Seafood School. These are particularly popular with women looking for unusual milestone birthday presents for their partner or husband.

Through looking at the creative tourism development experiences of countries around the world it will help destinations and operators in the UK develop their own offer. Several examples are provided in a book compiled from presentations given at a creative tourism conference in Santa Fe 2008 .

A different experience is described by Caroline Couret who is responsible for Barcelona Creative Tourism (BCT). Funded by La Fundació Societat i Cultura (FUSIC) a non-profit cultural organisation. BCT launched in 2006 and acts as a facilitator, matching 'creative tourists' with cultural and creative activities through www.barcelonacreativa.info.

The organisation develops customised solutions for creative tourists; from those who wish to develop their artistic skills to those with more sophisticated projects, for example an orchestra in London who wishes to organise a concert. Their assistance ranges from providing advice and information to event design and technical production, as well as tailormade creative itineraries.

Examples given include those of helping a French band who wished to learn Catalan rumba music originating in Barcelona; BCT created a programme that also included jam sessions with a local group. They also organised a stay for art students who wanted to work with Barcelona creatives, which included an exhibition of their own work.

In effect BCT act as a ground handler for creative tourism in Barcelona whilst being subsidised by public funds.

New Zealand

One of the most illuminating examples is the experience of Creative Tourism New Zealand (CTNZ). It was started in 2003 by Crispin Raymond and Greg Richards who are credited with first identifying and naming creative tourism.

The creative workshops were delivered by tutors in their own homes in Nelson, on South Island, an area already known for its thriving arts community. Subjects included bronze casting, bone carving and seafood cookery. Despite hard work and persistence and enthusiasm from those who attended, the lack of a clearly targeted marketing campaign resulted in insufficient participants to make the project financially viable in the longer term.

CTNZ is currently considering whether to seek additional private capital and work with an established tourism partner with existing tourism distribution or whether to establish a Trust and develop a wider community network and seek more public funding.

Current UK Offers

Some tour operators already using creative pursuits in the UK as part of their offer and include Warner Holidays, Saga and lastminute.com who are offering a range of creative activities from 'Strictly Ballroom' dancing breaks, to song writing and recording, chocolate making, wine appreciation and safari park photography.

There are examples of non-residential Arts Centres providing creative workshops and that appear to be considering and promoting to visitor markets and linking to accommodation and other tourism providers. These include Craft in the Bay in Cardiff, home of the Makers Guild of Wales, offering one to three day creative workshop breaks to a maximum group size of 8 and New Brewery Arts in Cirencester.

Residential centres for creative breaks in England include; Farncombe, near Broadway in the Cotswolds and Flatford Mill, close to the Suffolk/Essex border West Dean in Sussex and Missenden Abbey in Buckinghamshire, and other members of Adult Residential Colleges.

Whilst some areas of the UK have pockets of creative tourism products, no single destination has yet developed a strong creative tourism profile. However, Herefordshire, on the border of England and Wales, is probably the most advanced in this respect.

The Creative Breaks Association was set up in 2000 with the assistance of Herefordshire Council to introduce visitors to Herefordshire to local artists and craftspeople. Creative Breaks - in and around Herefordshire offer more than 300 courses, workshops and holidays on topics ranging from crafts and painting to cooking and earth oven building.

Northumberland Tourism is exploring creative tourism and in 2009 worked with Made in Northumberland to bring tourism providers together with artists. Visit Northumberland includes pages devoted to Northumberland crafts and a link to the Northumberland artists and crafters network, some of whom deliver workshops.

KENT'S CREATIVE COAST

Visit Kent is currently working with Campbell on the Create in Kent programme to position the county as the place to be creative in the UK, and in particular to develop the Kent's Creative Coast brand.

The aim is to encourage positive perceptions of Kent's Coast, to increase visitor spend and seasonality, for the benefit of tourism providers, the creative communities and the wider Kent economy.

The programme comprises the following.

1. Business training and coaching to support and encourage:

" creative individuals and groups who wish to develop taster creative workshops

" tourism businesses (including food producers such as vineyards) who wish to appeal to visitors interested in creative tourism products.

2. Facilitation to develop creative tourism products.

3. Promotion of creative tourism products through their website, blog, Twitter and other social, e-marketing and media relations.

As a first step in the development of the programme, a creative tourism workshop was organised in November 2009, for creative professionals and tourism providers from destinations along the coast to communicate the opportunities presented by creative tourism and to encourage partnership working. The response was excellent from both tourism and arts delegates and training is planned for early 2010 with the aim to have creative tourism products ready for promotion later this year.

Some of the ideas being developed include:

" hotel accommodation combined with an arts or crafts workshop

" watercolour painting in a stately home

" stone carving or sculpture in the grounds of a castle

" cookery workshops using Kent produce in farmhouses, vineyards or restaurant

" walking and cycling tours with photography tuition.

Creative tourism development around the world, including the UK, shows that it has mainly been driven by arts providers and public funding, and when this money dries up, projects have found it difficult to continue. For creative tourism in the UK to be successful it needs to be driven by the tourism sector that has existing routes to market and business development expertise.

The benefits of creative tourism for tourism providers include the opportunities to enhance existing cultural experiences and to provide differentiation from the competition. For destinations it not only offers opportunities to provide local authentic experiences and to extend the season, but also delivers additional economic benefits to creative professionals delivering the learning experiences and for the wider community living and working there.

Even with the current downturn in the economy many people still feel that a holiday is fundamental. A break that combines the opportunity to learn a new skill and take home a unique souvenir, a change of scene in high-quality accommodation in a distinctive location, and the sharing of an experience with people with a common interest, can provide a competitive edge for many destinations.

What is the Right Time to Travel Costs Less

Traveling is really a wonderful experience as it helps us to explore beautiful locations, historical places and unimaginable destinations. It is often seen that if you are traveling to a particular destination at the right time of the year, it can really cost you very less. If you travel during off seasons, you will see a marked difference in the cost of all the things.

Summer and the spring seasons are often considered to be the peak seasons of most of the places unless it a totally snow covered region. Other than saving many you have many other advantages while traveling during the off seasons.

During the off seasons you will find a fewer number of tourists and crowd on the street and the shopping area. This would help you to visit all the destinations of interest in a much enjoyable and peaceful manner.

So, now let us discuss how traveling at the right time of the years helps you in saving your costs.

1. You can save on accommodations

Accommodation costs are generally very high during the peak seasons. There are so many tourists visiting the popular destination that you would find crown all around. Even getting the booking in a decent hotel or resort becomes difficult. While you are traveling during the off seasons you will get all sought of discounts on lodging, recreational facilities and food. So, if you are on budget you must always travel during the off peak seasons.

2. Air fares are considerably cheaper

During the off seasons mostly very less people prefer to fly as compared to that of peak seasons. During the off seasons there is a lot of completion among different airlines; hence they drop their prices to a considerable extent in order to attract customers. If you are booking your vacation through a travel agency you can even get another added benefit from it.

3. Local traveling becomes easier

During the off seasons, as there are fewer crowds in popular destinations, you can easily avail discounts on your traveling passes. You can even get discount on tickets of amusement parks and other such places of interest.

4. Eating also becomes cheaper

Many travelers tend to spend a lot of money on eating items. These items can cost you a fortune if you are staying at and expensive hotel during the peak seasons. So, visiting during the off peak seasons can be very beneficial for you because many restaurant owner give excellent discounts in order to attract visitors.

ALASKAADVENTURE TRAVELING

Alaska is a place where you can enjoy many adventurous activities. If you have ever dreamed of an Alaskan vacation, you can experience the excitement and breathtaking beauty with Great

Alaska Adventure tours. So, now let us discuss about some Alaska Adventure Travelling tours.

1.Alaska backpacking and trekking trips

Alaska backpacking and trekking trips can really be very exciting if you are with family and friends. You can experience hidden valleys, glaciers, sweeping Alaskan vistas, wildlife and much more while trekking the majestic mountains of Wrangell-St. Elias National Park.

2.Alaska Bicycling tours

You can experience magnificent mountains, salmon filled rivers, calving glaciers, abundant wildlife and Alaska's pristine sidetracked while on a bicycling tours because they are very exciting and adventurous.

3.Alaskan rafting tours

If you have never experience rafting then Alaska is the place for your. Many rafting tour companies offer different types of facilities to the tourists, which are both interesting and breathtaking. Experience the wild cascades, gigantic waves while on a river rafting tour.

4.Alaska dog sledging tours

Since 1976, Alaska Dog Sledding has specialized in small group wilderness, Alaska adventure travel and dog mushing trips into some of Alaska's most beautiful and remote locations with lodge and deluxe safari style accommodations. So, come and enjoy this thrilling experience.

5.Alaska Eagle and Bird watching tours

On these tours you can get up close and personal with Alaskan bears, eagles and birds. These tours offer a range of camp based nature tours and coastal treks in Alaska's Katmai National Park. They focus on wildlife and nature photography, eagle/bird watching, and Alaskan bear viewing.

6.Alaskan Mountaineering and hiking Tours

You can plan an Alaskan vacation for your family and friends, climb Denali, film a movie or organize your own expedition. Alaska kayaking, glacier hiking, ice climbing, mountaineering, backpacking, multi-sport and other types of Alaska adventures are featured in this tour.

7.Alaska Flight seeing Tours

In this tour you can see glacier filled valleys, ice fields, limestone canyons and the fabulous mountain peaks of Wrangell-St. Elias National Park, these are the only things that make these tours comparable to the best Alaskan flight seeing anywhere. This would be a very unique and unusual stuff for you and your family members.

8.Alaska Photography Tour

Alaska Photography Tours are one and two-day tours that are intended to explore some of the local photographic hot spots while learning the art of photography. Here you can click all the photographs that you want in order to keep the memories of this beautiful place alive for ever.

These are some Alaska adventure tours that would surely make your vacations in Alaska very pleasant.

Lanzarote, a Spanish island which is made up of volcanic eruptions, is the easternmost of the Canary Islands, in the Atlantic Ocean, roughly covering an area of 125 km off the coast of Africa and 1,000 km from the Iberian Peninsula. It covers a large area and is the fourth largest of the islands. The island's name in the native language was Titerroygatra, which means "the red mountains".

This island is a very beautiful place and thousands of tourists come here every year from all around the world. This island has an exclusive mixture of fantastic volcanic caves and craters, breathtaking beaches and all year-round sunshine. Here you can see very unusual sights and scenes like the fertile agricultural fields among creepy formations of terrified lava, beaches of black volcanic sand and vineyards growing in the very center of volcanic craters.

Lanzarote also known as 'Conejera' by the natives is also called the island of 100 volcanoes. Its volcanic origin has created a landscape with more than 300 volcanoes. But this exotic island is the best for having summer fun filled activities. The palm trees, almost the only kind of native tree life found here grow in the banks of the barrancos and the bottoms of the valleys.

There are many places that you can visit in this island. Some of the places are La Cueva de los Verdes, Mirador del Río, Jameos del Agua, The Jardín de Cactus, International Museum of Contemporary Art, The National Park of Timanfaya and El Monumento a La Fecundidad. All these places are very exciting and can be visited by the tourists while they are in Lanzarote.

There are also many beaches which the visitors must see in order to enjoy their visit to the fullest. Some of the famous beaches of this place are Las Cucharas beach, Costa Teguise beaches, and Los Charcos and Bastian beaches, Beaches at Orzola, Beaches at Arrieta, El Reducto, El Cable, Guacimeta beach, Playa Honda beach, Playa Blanca, Playa de Los Pocillos, Playa de Matagorda, Caleta de Caballo, La Santa beach and Papagayo beaches.

The centre place of this island is a beautiful, azure lake populated by a rare species of blind, albino crab. There are bars and a restaurant around the lake, swimming pools and a concert hall with the seating for 500 people.

This island also has many exotic resorts, like the Playas de las Americas and Los Cristianos. So, if you really want to enjoy a fun filled summer under the sun, visit this place.

Outdoor activities are enjoyed by adventuresome people and travel geeks. Traveling to adventurous places is liked by many people and the excitement and thrill involved in uncommon outdoor activities is enjoyed by travelers. There is a long list of outdoor activities enjoyed by the travelers but uncommon outdoor activities are not easy to embark by every people. You can search for the uncommon outdoor activity for preparing the list and then outdoor activities can be chosen according to the i9nterest and budget. Some outdoor activities are quite dangerous and cannot be chosen by everyone.

Following are uncommon outdoor adventures:

1. There are many places in different parts of the world where you can plan the vacations for mining. Valuable rocks are present in different places and it is quite interesting to search the rocks having valuable stones and gems. You have to select the place where there is no danger and rocks are found in plethora containing stones.
2. You can carry the metal detectors for finding the precious metals like gold in the rocks. Sometimes if the luck favors then adventure trip can be profitable too. Quartz and precious metals are found in the places if your choice of selection of destination point is perfect.
3. There are many natural pools formed by the rivers flowing in the mountain regions which are preferred by the travelers to enjoy in the beautiful places. People like to enjoy boating and swimming in the canyons. Canyons also have the potential of fishing and it is enjoyed by people. Powerful boats along the steep slopes and reefs make the journey of canyons interesting.
4. Rafting trips are liked by many people and there are many rivers famous for the rafting trips. The scenic beauty around the places win the heart of people and also exciting journey of rafting trip is mind blowing.
5. Camping trips near to the places having fishes in plethora is enjoyed by travelers. Fishing is interesting outdoor activity which can be enjoyed in the places having variety of fishes in abundance.
6. Mountain flying is popular outdoor activity which is enjoyed by people. There are many places in US which are famous for mountain flying. You just have to contact the flying clubs by keeping the budget in mind.

Travel geeks like to spend beautiful vacations in the spring season in different parts of the world. There are many sensational destinations for spending lovely vacations without any hassle. You can search the internet and can find the list of destination spots for getting the favorable spring season. Many people like to plan the trip to dazzling beaches of the world and some prefer places with scenic beauty. The activities preferred by travelers can also play important role in deciding the place for travel. Outdoor activities and recreational activities are offered by many places to tourists preferring entertaining vacations.

Following pointers describe about the top spring break destinations:

1. Students' living in America likes to go for party in the awesome places for spending week off. Millions of students choose the spring season months for partying hard on incredible locations. Beaches like Panama City in Florida are popular among students for spending exciting holidays. All sorts of facilities are available for entertainment and amusement park is the center of attraction. Vibrant nightlife is enjoyed by the tourists.
2. Cruises are becoming more popular among students for spending great vacations. Caribbean islands are one of the best places for cruise vacations. Fantastic climate of the islands attract large numbers of travelers to spend lovely vacations and enjoy outdoor activities with water sports and beach side sports.
3. Cancun is one of the hot spot in Mexico where people like to plan the vacations due to pleasant climate. Natural beauty galore and there are many exciting spots for enjoying the day and night life. Although Cancun tour is little expensive but it is preferred by people for enjoying to the fullest.
4. Travelers who love skiing like to visit West Virginia for skiing vacations on the awesome skiing grounds. Skiing grounds attract travelers and also the market area full of life is the center of attraction in West Virginia. You can get variety of drinks and delicious food in bars and pubs.
5. There is no need to visit from places around your city for enjoying the spring break but you can participate in volunteering

in different activities of your choice. You can engage yourself in social work and it depicts your good character on resume. There are many places which can be easily found in the vicinity to volunteer for good cause.

Helpful Tips When to Go on a Cheap Cruise Vacation

Cruise vacation has its own importance and popularity among various tourists as it provides them the real cruise experience surrounded with the gigantic ocean, exploring islands, fully engaged in water sports and other activities. The luxury is the basic reason why everybody wants to go on a cruise vacation. It provides number of facilities such as a perfect and comfortable stay, with delicious food served in the restaurants, full of people from various parts of the world, enjoying and having a chill out in the discos and pubs inside the Cruise. Apart from that you also get spa and fitness centers with various sport courts, swimming pools and a fascinating shopping experience in there.

The main thing that everybody thinks is of the budgeted cruise vacations which become impossible for the family fun as they can be expensive at times. So if you all want some helpful tips to know when to go on a cheap cruise vacation which suits your budget.

The rate of cheap cruise trips consists of: -

1. Air travel i.e. from airplane or seaplane
2. The cruise rate
3. Attractions on the cruise with the breakfast, lunch and dinner facilities with varieties of food
4. Along with that some evening snacks, with best room services
5. Other features such as rates for the gym, spas or swimming pools and various other forms of entertainment.
6. The cheap cruise vacations gives us the normal and a comfortable stay giving a large window with sea side view or a usual room with bright natural light.
7. We can also choose those cheap cruises which make us go and explore the nearby beautiful islands such as the cheap

royal Caribbean Cruises. We can also go and stay on the beach or enjoy the bonfire parties at night with a romantic air blowing and get back to the cruise ships.

8. We should not forget to bring our passport and other documents. Though the cruising is the safest journey but the main things should not be avoided. Apart from that cheap cruise trips are basically informal but some shows or parties need you to wear those formal outfit. Keep your medical kits with you in order to avoid sea sickness or fevers. And you should do your travel insurance done to stay relaxed even if your belongings get lost.

9. The shopping or even movie seeing in the theaters can become costly in the luxury cruise trips but it is up to you how you make your cruise planning and how you all manage your budget.

The above tips are very useful for going on a cheap Cruise vacation. But before you all go to have a mind blowing experience and charismatic view of the gorgeous islands and ocean, check out the cheap and best travel packages to make your vacation a memorable moments to share and capture your heart.

Mexico also called as the City of Palaces is the most attractive, most complex and the cosmopolitan city which is surrounded by the mountains. It is bordered on the north by the United States; on the south and west by the North Pacific Ocean; on the southeast by Guatemala, and the Caribbean Sea; and on the east side by the Gulf of Mexico.

In Mexico you will see the typical art and architecture, diverse culture and traditions with lots of customs just to make your trip a memorable one. It is composed of everything from beautiful beaches to museums to opera houses and lots more just to take your heart away.

The climate of Mexico is totally different. The northern half will be cooler in winters but the southern half will have that constant temperature.

Mexico is the appealing country and has diverse attractions and festivals to see and love and it is famous for the ruins of various civilizations thus becoming the famous tourist destination.

1. Rio Grande Rivers are the famous hotspots for every traveler to enjoy their vacations. As Mexico is famous for the beautiful rivers and Rio Grande is the biggest of all. Thus popular for the adventure seeking tourists.
2. There are 2 mountain ranges thus famous for adventurous people who want to do trekking and camping or try out their favorite sports such as bungee jumping. They are known as Sierra Madre Occidental and Sierra Madre Oriental having natural height and splendor.
3. Another famous place to visit is the Oaxaca Plateau in the southwest part of Mexico which is famous for ancient remains of the olden city built by old civilization.
4. As it is rightly said that beaches are the famous part of Mexico so the splendid famous beach is the Isla Mujeres which adds to its beauty with the help of surrounded Caribbean Sea. There you will also find white sandy beaches to make yourself occupy in participating various water sports or just basking in the sun and making sand castles.
5. Bull fighting is the major cultural events which has gained its popularity since olden cultural times.
6. Mexicans even love to celebrate their festivals with great pomp and show. It is Day of the Dead or El Dia de los Muertos festival to remember the passed away. It is seen that people celebrate this festival by making sweets and other dishes in the shape of skeleton.
7. The cathedrals in Mexico are also a great place to offer prayers to God and the famous altarpiece is Nuestra Señora del Carmen as the "doorway of angels".
8. Other famous place is to see the Maya City of Tulum which reminds us of the ancient marvelous beauty of Maya civilization.

CHAPTER 6

NORMS TO ETIQUETTES AND MANNERISM FOR TOURISTS

No hugging and kissing, no wearing short clothes and no discussion on religion in India. Public toilets are very few and filthy, so carry your own tissues papers here and always take your shoes off before entering a house in India.

These lessons on etiquettes and a plethora of travel tips is what the Commonwealth Games Organising committee has put up in its website for the tourists who are planning to travel to India during the Delhi Games from October 3-14.

In its 'Travelers Zone' section, the OC have given a list of tips on 18 varied topics ranging from Visa to Toilets, besides a separate point on 'some important dos and don'ts'.

"The Western practice of a peck on the cheek as a form of greeting a lady or a grown up girl is JUST NOT DONE when you are in India unless you happen to be in 'Westernized Indian' circles ... If you find the lady is not extending a hand shake, go for the Namastey," reads one of the advisories.

"Be aware that public displays of affection (hugging, kissing) are generally not appreciated. However, it is common to see men showing affection and camaraderie on the roads and in villages throughout the country," it added.

The website also gives tips on a dress code and what one should do if one visits a house in India.

"Modesty in dress is an important aspect of Indian life and, away from beaches, one should respect the local customs. This is especially important when visiting temples and religious sites, where trousers or full-length skirts should be worn and shoulders should be covered and in Sikh temples, your head must also be covered.

"If somebody has invited you home for dinner, carry with you a bottle of wine accompanied by a bouquet of flowers or at least a box of sweets or chocolate bars for the children ... People usually take their shoes off before entering a house and putting feet on the furniture is considered bad manners," it reads.

There are also tips of eating behaviour and what to discuss in public.

"Politics can be freely discussed in India and most people will have an opinion which they will not mind being contradicted, but avoid discussing religion.

"If eating Indian style, with the hands, it is useful to remember that it is considered impolite to use the left hand for eating," it says.

But of all the tips, one that takes the cake is lessons on Indian toilets for the travellers.

"In India, public toilet facilities are few and far between and, outside of the hotels and restaurants, can be of dubious cleanliness. We recommend taking every opportunity you can to use a clean toilet in hotels and restaurants and that you carry tissues/wet wipes with you," it reads.

Also if you thought of driving in the Indian roads, think twice because it is India and traffic congestion here can give you a torrid time.

"For your safety, we suggest that you do not hire transportation from unlicensed or unapproved operators. We can provide you all types of transportation at very reasonable prices. Self-driven cars, though available, are not recommended as it is not advisable for you to drive on the Indian roads with all the traffic," it read.

Indians are curious by nature, so if you are stared at, please don't mind. It is just curiosity, says another tip.

"Even in the most cosmopolitan of cities in India the chances are that your different appearance might mean that you will be stared at, though this especially happens in the smaller towns and more remote areas. Please do not be offended, no harm is meant, it is just curiosity," the advisory adds.

TRAVEL ETIQUETTE IN SINGAPORE

Singapore being one of the most urbanized nations of the world marks the visit of a large number of tourists every year. Every nation has some unique features of their own and the visitors are expected to follow the traditional travel etiquettes to create a good impression. Since time immemorial it has been a tradition followed by the discerning travelers to remain adhere to the basic travel etiquettes for a memorable journey. Travel etiquette is some of the special norms that a traveler is expected to follow while getting around a foreign nation or staying there for a short period of time.

Singapore is a multi-religious nation and people from all religions reside here. The tourists are expected to show full respect to the various religious groups present in Singapore. The travelers in Singapore mainly for business purposes are advised to be punctual while visiting formal meetings and conferences. The Singapore businessmen are well known for maintaining a high standard of punctuality level. The men travelers are expected to maintain the decency level while conversing with Singaporean women. The visitors are advised to remain tactful and indulge moderately with the local people. The custom laws in Singapore are very severe and the tourists are expected to remain adhere to the local laws. The narcotic laws can even lead an accused to face the death penalty. Smoking is not allowed in the air-conditioned areas of Singapore. Littering and jaywalking is also taken to be an offense in Singapore. The tourists are advised not to spend much in tipping, as it is not taken to be a respected practice in Singapore. The travelers are advised not to carry any restricted items with them.

Take care of your own belongings and never leave it on charge of any unknown person.

In Japan, there are more opportunities for making etiquette mistakes than you can shake a chopstick at -- hang on, better not do that, it may cause offense. For every Japanese etiquette mistake listed here, there are another 50 that could have your face turning as red as a Japanese plum.

To help smooth things along and keep that all-important social harmony intact, we've compiled a list of 10 Japanese etiquette mistakes you really don't want to make. You'll be pleased to know, however, that Japanese folk are generally pretty generous toward the non-Japanese who don't know the rules, so don't spend too much time worrying about the occasional indiscretion -- and be sure to enjoy yourself.

Blowing Your Nose in Public

In a crowded public place like a train car, emptying the contents of your nostrils into a tissue or, worse, a handkerchief is a big no-no in Japan. You're better off doing what many others do -- sniffing a lot. Every train car has its sniffers and, occasionally, some snorters too. If you must honk into your hanky, just do it as discreetly as you possibly can and try not to spend too much time gawking at the fruits of your labor once the job is done.

Pointing With Your Forefinger

It may not be the worst faux pas you can make, but pointing with your forefinger at the person you're talking to may cause them to feel a little uncomfortable -- even threatened. It's the kind of thing you might do without realizing, although the troubled look on the other person's face -- as if you've just pulled a loaded revolver on them -- should alert you to the fact that something's not quite right. If you must point, try clenching your fist, using your thumb as the pointy bit.

Pouring Your Own Beer When out with Friends

Serving others is big in Japan, even when you're three sheets to the wind with your drinking buddies down your local izakaya. If you're drinking beer that's being poured from bottles, then impress your fellow diners by topping them up. They'll surely reciprocate. If you try to pour your own, you'll be set upon by a flock of flapping hands, at which point you can humbly relinquish the bottle and allow someone to pour for you. Following this, it's a good move to top up other people's drinks if you spot any half-full glasses.

Wearing the Toilet Slippers Back to Your Seat

This is a slippery one. Whether it's in someone's home or in a restaurant, when nature calls, there'll likely be a pair slippers waiting for you at the entrance to the bathroom. Slip out of your other slippers into the toilet slippers, do your business and then be sure to slip out of the toilet slippers and back into your original slippers. Don't worry, you won't be the first person (nor the last) to wear the toilet slippers back to your seat, but it will be noticed. The question is: Will anyone point it out to you? Or perhaps you'll suddenly notice before slipping discreetly back to the bathroom to slip back into your original slippers in an effort to cover up your slightly embarrassing slipup.

Giving Gifts in Multiples of Four

As in many other cultures, there are quite a few social indiscretions connected with death. In the Japanese language, the sound of the word for "four" is the same as the word for "death," therefore, it comes as little surprise that four is regarded as an unlucky number. As a result, if you've been invited to someone's home, giving four of something as a gift will likely make the recipient feel a little awkward; so, you're best to stick with a safer number -- like five.

In a Public Bath, Failing to Wash First

Public baths are a great place to scrub up before taking a long, relaxing soak. Just make sure you do it in that order. Entering the bathing area and making a beeline for the bath before you've polished your privates (as well as the rest of your body) is not going to put you in the best light. As you enter the main bathing area from the changing room, you'll see an area close by where you can sit on a little stool and scrub up, with all the necessary accoutrements at your fingertips. Don't forget that the bath is for soaking and you should smell of roses before you join your fellow bathers in the communal water.

Passing food from your chopsticks to someone else's

The only acceptable time to pass something between two people using chopsticks is at a funeral: Following the cremation, the remaining bones of the deceased are picked up by a relative using special chopsticks and passed to the chopsticks held by another relative who then places the bones into the urn. So keep that in mind when you're having dinner in a restaurant and you're thinking of passing your leftovers to a friend. Better to place it directly onto their plate rather than remind someone in your dining party of the passing of a loved one.

Sticking your chopsticks upright in a bowl of rice

This is also connected with Japanese funeral rites. If you're in a restaurant or eating at home, the sight of a pair of chopsticks sticking up out of a bowl of rice is something no one will be pleased to see. It may even cause an audible gasp. At Buddhist funerals in Japan, this is how rice is offered to the dead and so, as with passing food between chopsticks, it could conjure up sad memories for others, or simply make some people feel uncomfortable. When you're not using them, place your chopsticks together on the rests and you'll save yourself a red face.

Mishandling someone's business card

It's not only in formal business situations that someone might offer you their card. It could happen whenever and wherever you strike up a conversation with a Japanese person, whether it's in a bar or down at the local park. Being a non-Japanese, you won't be expected to observe all of the intricate rules of a business card exchange, though you can still get brownie points by giving it the respect it deserves. Taking it with both hands looks good, and spending a little time showing an interest in it is a real plus, during which the giver will probably confirm his/her name if you're not sure of it already. Whatever you do, don't write on it, fold it or stuff it in your back pocket. Simply place it carefully in your wallet or card holder.

Wearing your shoes into someone's home

As noted in the introduction, the Japanese are generally pretty forgiving when it comes to visitors making a mess of things in the etiquette department. There's one thing, however, that may literally be a step too far. Crossing over the threshold of someone's home wearing your soiled shoes or boots instead of discarding them in the genkan (entranceway) may, to put it mildly, place something of a strain on your relationship with the proud homeowner. If you really want to ingratiate yourself, as you enter, say "ojama shimasu" ("sorry to disturb you") and then be sure to remove your footwear. There'll most likely be a pair of slippers waiting for you, which incidentally also act as a useful prompt for you to take off your shoes. Oh, and be sure to wear socks that aren't riddled with holes!

Business etiquette tips for expats in Dubai

While carrying out business in any foreign workplace, it is necessary that certain norms relating to etiquettes followed by that country should be embedded within us. Known officially as 'Business etiquettes' these norms follow different rules in each country.

Working Hours: Dubai is one of the seven emirates in the UAE located in the Mid East region. Topically it is known to face harsh summers with temperatures rising to boiling points. Due to this taking a break between working hours is a common practice in all Dubai offices. A typical working week in Dubai proceeds from Saturday to Wednesday with the working day starting at 8:00 pm till 1:00 pm. Afternoon hours from 2:00 pm to 5:00 pm are siesta times after which business recommences at 5:00 pm and runs till 7:00 pm in the evening. During Ramadan working days are two hours shorter.

Formal Dress Code: Although the most liberal of all emirates, Dubai still follows a silent and assumed dress code that adheres to mild conservatism. Business suits for men and formal office wear like jackets & trousers for women is essential as covered arms and legs are termed as appropriate. Women should dress conservatively refraining from short skirts and low necklines when on business. If you are working in rural Dubai, dress up in their traditional attire.

Casual Conversations: Business meetings with Arab clients can take place in informal places such as restaurants. The conversation generally starts by inquiring about the family and making a polite chat; say about the Dubai weather. It's possible that you may quickly arrive at the formal business conversation part with the meeting getting over in a shorter period of time than stipulated.

Keep controversies apart: Don't criticize an Arab business colleague or start a controversy regarding business or personal matters, in public places. This will be termed as an 'insult' of the colleague which will be resented by him.

An Arab Handshake: Arab handshakes are very gentle compared to the West. Just the touching of the palms of the right hands is fine. Call the colleague by 'Mr' (Sayed) or 'Mrs' (Sayeda) if a woman. Don't initiate a handshake with a woman, unless she offers to do so.

Business Cards: Have one side of your business card translated in Arabia as a gesture of politeness. While presenting your business card to an Arab colleague/client keep the Arabic side of the card face up.

Business Dining Etiquette

Business executives are constantly on their toes when dealing with important clients or business partners. Formal dinners can be rather - pressurizing in situations where executives need to demonstrate their best efforts, whether it is proper communication, dress code, or dining etiquettes. A few tips kept in mind will certainly help in tiding over the hardest of situations and securing a business deal for your company.

Dining manners are an important part of business etiquette as most of the deals, interviews and meeting are cracked over the dinner table. Whether dinner is at an elegant restaurant or at a formal corporate dining hall, it does not matter, as long as table manners are meticulously followed. The following tips will certainly mark the boundaries of Dining Etiquette:

Do's

1. Arrive on time. If you are going to be late, make sure to inform your client or business partner.
2. Dress conservatively.
3. After sitting down, quietly unfold your napkin and place it on your lap. Fold it in half and place the folded half towards your waist.
4. Before starting with the dinner, wait for all your client or business partners to arrive
5. Turn off cell phones and pagers while dining.
6. Maintain proper upright posture while dining.
7. Keep elbows off the table.
8. If confused about ordering the meal, let the host decide.
9. Order simple menu items eaten with a knife and fork, chopsticks, or other utensils. Avoid finger foods.
10. Start your meal after everyone starts his or hers.
11. Use both knife and fork together to cut your food.
12. Taste your meal before making any additions.
13. Eat in small bites and try to finish your dinner at the same time as everyone else.
14. Stir your soup gently from the farthest edge, instead of blowing it. Drink soup from the edge of the spoon and not putting the whole spoon in your mouth.

15. If bread is in the shape of a loaf, tear it with hands and not a knife.
16. If you have something in your mouth that you cannot swallow, inconspicuously remove it with your fork.
17. If you want to bring a problem to the waiter's attention, do it discreetly.
18. After finishing your meal, place napkin to the left of the plate. The knife and fork should be placed in the centre of the plate in the five a clock position. The waiter will know that you have finished with your meal.
19. Decide beforehand how the bill is going to be paid
20. Tip 15% for moderate service and 20% for excellent service. Tip charges may differ according to location and country.

DON'TS

1. Do not hurry to know the arrival status of your clients. Wait at least 15 minutes before calling up.
2. Do not put bags, briefcases, and other accessories on the table.
3. Do not change the order of dining utensils placed on the table.
4. Do not reshuffle the order of dining utensils according to your handedness.
5. Do not order expensive menu items or alcohol at business meals.
6. Do not apply make up at the table.
7. Do not bite on ice or talk when mouth is full.
8. Do not slurp soups or drinks or make noises while chewing food.

Chapter 7

CREATIVE MIND GIVES YOU AN EDGE TO FELLOW TRAVELLERS

I see them all the time: the Los Angeles tourist who's made a mistake. They're stuck in traffic on the 405, shivering in their shorts at the beach or paying too much for their hotel room. To help you be a smarter Los Angeles tourist, enjoy your trip more and spend less of your hard-earned money doing it, try these Los Angeles tourist tips:

Eight Ways to be a Smart Los Angeles Tourist

1. Know the Weather: Baywatch was filmed in Los Angeles, and summer weather can be quite warm here. However, it always cools off at the beach in late afternoon, winter can be rainy and the "June gloom" marine layer often obscures the sun for weeks at a time. Our guide to weather and what to expect can help you bring the right stuff.
2. Avoid the 405: This freeway seems to be perpetually gridlocked, especially between US 101 and Long Beach, and you can get in a traffic jam on it anytime, whether it's rush hour, midnight on Tuesday or noon on Sunday. Get a good map and use it to plot another route. Use the guide to getting around Los Angeles, which may also help. Depending on where

you are and where you're going, consider using the Metro Rail instead of driving.

3. Get a Hotel Bargain: If you're willing to invest some time, you can get excellent weekend rates in the Los Angeles area, especially in the hotels south of LAX in El Segundo that cater to weekday business travelers such as the Hilton Garden Inn. The Priceline bidding strategies that work well in other locations don't seem to net such good bargains here, and you'll often get a better price by booking directly through a hotel website.

4. Know the Geography: The Los Angeles metropolitan area is a big place, encompassing five counties and it can take almost all day to drive across it from north to south. You can attack it in two ways: (1) Figure out what you want to do while you're here, mark the locations on a map and visit them in groups, or (2) pick an area to stay in such as Hollywood or the beach cities and visit the attractions in that area.

5. You Have Options for Airports: While Los Angeles International Airport (LAX) is the best-known and busiest airport in the area, it's also prone to delays, busy and confusing. Consider flying into Burbank (BUR), Orange County's John Wayne Airport (SNA) or Long Beach (LGB) instead.

6. What to Expect in Hollywood and Beverly Hills: What you will find in Hollywood are museums featuring memorabilia from Hollywood's past, the Walk of Fame and the famous footprints at Grauman's Chinese Theater. Few movie stars live here, or in Beverly Hills, and most of the studios moved out years ago. Skip the overpriced movie star home tours and don't buy the maps you'll find sold on the roadside either. Frankly, they're mostly fiction. If you realy want to see a star or two, the most reliable way to do it is to get a reservation to watch a television show taping.

7. Go to the Beach: Beaches typify Los Angeles and Southern California in many people's minds. While the water's a little too cold for all the but the hardiest swimmers or surfers in

wetsuits, it doesn't keep people from flocking to the sand. Join the locals to watch the beach volleyball games while you stroll along the beachside sidewalks in Manhattan Beach, Hermosa Beach or Rendondo Beach, where you'll be joined by rollerbladers, bicyclists and runners; visit Venice Beach for a taste of the unusual, or head to Orange County's Newport Beach or Huntington Beach for surfing and sand castles.

8. Save Money on Admissions: If you're visiting several attractions with admission fees, look the companies offering multi-attraction discount packs. Offering fewer attractions (but ones that you are most likely to want to see) is Citypass. You can buy their Southern California Pass or Hollywood Citypass online before you go to save time later. The Go Los Angeles Card offers a lot of things to do, but be sure you'll use enough of them to make it worthwhile before you purchase.

Sure, we all know Paris is a big city with it's fair share of petty crime - even the announcements in the Metro stations warn tourists to "faire attention aux pickpockets."

But aside from just generally watching your wallet or purse, there are a number of scams typically used on tourists in Paris. They should know it's not so easy to con a Cheapo!

Here are a few of the most typical scams to watch out for:

1. "Free" bracelets at Sacre Coeur

Most days, as tourists start to walk up the steps to reach Sacre Coeur, they face a veritable gauntlet of men trying to trick them out of a few euros. This scam involves someone tying a string bracelet onto your wrist and then refusing to let go until you "pay" for the souvenir.

While these men can be aggressive, they are fairly easy to avoid. Often if you speak French they just leave you alone - a simple "non, merci" should do the trick.

2. "Did you drop this gold ring I just found?"

I don't really understand how this one works, but it must, because so many scammers still do it. It starts like this: as you're walking along the street, someone approaches you and asks, "Excuse me, did you drop this gold ring?" When you say, no, that's not mine, the person then tries to foist the ring on you, saying it must be worth a lot of money.

Since he or she is in the country illegally, the person can't possible sell the ring, but you as a respectable tourist should have no problem. Can you just give him or a her a little money (not even the value of the ring)? Of course, in reality the ring is worthless. Be on the lookout for this scam in the Jardin des Tuileries and the Champs de Mars, near the Eiffel Tower.

3. "Do you speak English?"

As foreigners in a strange land, we've all needed to ask for assistance at some point. So when someone asks if you speak English, the logical response is: "Yes, I do! How can I help?" However, the next step on the part of the asker is to hold up a card with a poorly written sob story asking for money.

This isn't so much a scam as a clever way to engage with tourists before begging for some spare change. It's up to you whether or not to part with a few euro coins. These alms seekers can be found in pretty much all the major tourist districts, and are especially abundant in the square facing Notre Dame.

Don't panic!

As the Hitchhiker's Guide to the Galaxy would tell you, don't panic! Like in any big city, it is important to remain on one's toes in Paris, but that shouldn't prevent you from having a good time. Just keep on eye on your belongings and use common sense and you should be fine!

Tell us your scam story

Have you witnessed or been the victim of a scam in Paris, or in any other city while traveling? Tell us about your experience- and what you've learned from it!

Among the 10 categories that hotel managers were quizzed on, Indians fared the worst on the politeness front. While the Japanese could not be faulted on their manners, Indians were rated the most impolite.

And with most Indian tourists travelling to Europe with their own chefs in tow, it is not a surprise that the European hospitality industry views them as the least interested in trying out local cuisine or sampling local specialities after the Italians.

"We ate Indian food everywhere because that's what the others on the tour wanted. Imagine eating chole-puri on Mount Titlis in Switzerland and being served samosas while watching Paris' famed Lido show! It was such a let down," said Bibli Das, who was on an European package tour last week.

Cleanliness does not seem to be a strong suit either, with those in the trade saying Indians leave their hotel rooms in a mess though they are not as messy as the Russians. The Germans were ranked as the tidiest.

It's gotten so bad that the US government has actually started issuing etiquette pamphlets for Americans traveling abroad, to try to clue them in on their behavior and how it ticks most of the world off. Unfortunately, most Americans seem to have missed the memo. So please, on behalf of Europe, let me ask the Americans to stop doing the following:

" Stop talking about how "cheap" everything is.

For starters, things aren't as cheap as you think they are, and most of you don't really have a clue about currency conversion. I hear people debating costs all the time. Bring a calculator, cos most of you cannot do the math in your heads. Secondly, if it is cheap, it may not be cheap to the people who live there and have to listen to you talk like you're King Midas. It's rude, so keep your remarks to yourself until your back in your hotel room.

" Stop talking so damned loud.

This is one of the most obnoxious things American tourists do. If you're in a bar where it's loud and you have be loud to hear yourself, great, go for it. But if you're in a nice restaurant, or club, or shop, etc. - shut up! Believe me, your conversations are not that interesting to the locals. And I mean that sincerely; it's ridiculous how petty the lot of you sound, said pettiness being yet another reason Europeans look down on us. Hard not to, really, when the biggest crisis in someone's life is running out of hairspray, and, ohmigod, like, will I be able to find Aquanet in this 3rd world country?

" Read something about the country you're visiting before you get on the plane.

Did you know that most Americans think the Czech Republic is still Czechoslovakia? John McCain is one of them. And, did you know that most who realize it isn't, think only the name has changed? And that those who realize it's now two separate countries, still don't realize the Czechs and Slovaks are two different peoples who speak two different languages? I've overheard seemingly educated people calling home on their cell phones to let mom know they're having a swell time in Czechoslovakia. Doh!

Do not assume people speak English.

Guess what? In the whole of Europe, the only place you're guaranteed to hear English, is in the UK. Do not waltz into Germany or France and expect the locals to speak English with you, and don't give them a dirty look if they can't. Most of the Europeans I know speak 3 languages, whether English is one of them or not. How many do you speak? Also, I see loads of Americans encounter non-English speakers.. and then start to speak more loudly. Or, they start speaking like they're addressing someone who is mentally challenged. Slick, people. Really, really slick.

" Don't assume people don't speak English.

Even if they say they can't speak English, most people do speak enough to understand whether or not you're speaking rudely about them. Just because the waitress doesn't know the name of that fancy drink you're asking for, doesn't mean she won't spit in your food while you snub her to your friends. Get some manners, or order room service.

" Don't ask people what communism/socialism was like, and don't pretend to understand it.

I've lived in a former soviet bloc country for 5 years. One which still has loads of red tape and an active communist party. Through having been accepted into a few local families, I've learned many things about life during communism/socialism - but I would never presume to understand what it was like. Which means some fool who just stepped off a plane shouldn't bring it up, either.

" Don't mention the Nazis when traveling through Germany.

Most Europeans still trash the Germans for the Nazis and they still toss words like Gestapo around - but not in Germany, they don't. Don't be an idiot. If I need to explain this one in detail, you're one of the Americans who ought to stay home.

" Don't get into pointless political arguments.

Whether you agree or disagree with American politics, don't get into it with the locals. Even if you agree with them, you're bound to make a fool of yourself, as most of them know more about your country's leaders and policies than you do. If you insist on debating anyway, please do it quietly so as not to embarrass the rest of us who have enough sense to just nod our agreement in silence.

" Don't "educate" people.

Don't try to explain life and other complexities to the locals; they're often quite educated and they tend to take school pretty seriously, even at a young age. Odds are, they're better read and better educated than most of you, so don't talk to them like you're addressing the deaf, dumb and blind kid, ok? As most of you just come off as condescending, whether you mean to, or not.

" Don't talk about how much better something is in America.

It's obnoxious. It's rude, and it's very, very American. That, and it's something you're unqualified to comment on unless you've actually lived in both. Yes, some things are better in the USA, and, believe it or not, some things are better in Europe. If you prefer the US, go home; Europe will be ok without you.

Obviously, this doesn't apply to ALL Americans. It does, however, apply to most. And, of course, it's not just Americans - the Brits do it too, but they're usually more subtle about it. At any rate, this kind of behavior does not reflect well on Americans, and is particularly annoying for those who actually live overseas, cos we get stuck having to assure the locals that not all Americans are so incredibly inept.

CHAPTER 8

TAKING SNAPS OF TOURIST PLACES

Whether it is a businessman who wants to know if it is safe to visit certain cities in Mexico or a tourist in Tokyo who suspects he has fractured his ankle, help is not far thanks to a service available to the Indian globe trotter.

The London and Singapore-based International SOS says its medical and security service promises corporates and tourists an emergency helpline service like the 911 in the US even in those parts f the globe where such assistance is tardy and hard to comy by.

Security advisories are part of the deal.

"When you travel outside the country, what is usually not a crisis at home can turn into a nightmare," said Laurent Sabourin, group managing director of International SOS. "This is where we come in," Sabourin told IANS.

The company said its operations span 70 countries with 66 percent of Fortune 500 firms availing themselves of its services, backed by a team of 6,000 employees, over 900 full-time physicians and more than 200 security specialists.

"All you need to do is to give our alarm centre a call, and we will get in touch with the local authorities or where such services are not present, in fact, arrange to get the person to the nearest medical facility," Sabourin said.

Such a service can indeed be life-saving for executives and travellers who are present in regions of conflict or which are so remote that medical help is almost always out of bounds.

International SOS's New Delhi alarm centre received over 90,000 calls during the last financial year from "in trouble" foreign nationals, ranging from the trivial toothache to more serious cases.

Tanguy de Grenier de Lassagne, country general manager of International SOS, says during the 26/11 terrorist attack in Mumbai the company's alarm centre and operatives calmed not only many clients but also other foreigners stuck in the terror-hit hotels.

"We catered to not only getting our members to safety, to hospitals, but also helped a lot of foreign nationals based on specific request from their missions," said Lassagne.

Now, with the advent of the Indian transnational corporations and their expanding span, human resource managers at these conglomerates, have to make sure their senior executives are safe whichever country they travel to.

Its client roster, the officials said boasts the crème de la crème of India Inc, but declined to name them individually due to confidentiality clauses on their pacts.

"People are not very much aware of the conditions in foreign countries. With Indian companies now spreading their geographical reach, they feel the need to take care of their people who are travelling abroad," said Sabourin.

He said such services are a big hit in many countries with even governments of countries like the US, Britain and Japan, as also UN agencies, soliciting assistance for diplomats or officials travelling to places where conditions are difficult, to say the least.

"Globalisation is main driver of our success. We were not affected even by recession. In fact companies that were eearlier hesitant to expand out of home markets were forced to do so, and we are there to help in advising on local security conditions."

CHAPTER 9

MEDICAL AND SECURITY SERVICE

Whether it is a businessman who wants to know if it is safe to visit certain cities in Mexico or a tourist in Tokyo who suspects he has fractured his ankle, help is not far thanks to a service available to the Indian globe trotter.

The London and Singapore-based International SOS says its medical and security service promises corporates and tourists an emergency helpline service like the 911 in the US even in those parts of the globe where such assistance is tardy and hard to comy by.

Security advisories are part of the deal.

"When you travel outside the country, what is usually not a crisis at home can turn into a nightmare," said Laurent Sabourin, group managing director of International SOS. "This is where we come in," Sabourin told IANS.

The company said its operations span 70 countries with 66 percent of Fortune 500 firms availing themselves of its services, backed by a team of 6,000 employees, over 900 full-time physicians and more than 200 security specialists.

"All you need to do is to give our alarm centre a call, and we will get in touch with the local authorities or where such services are not present, in fact, arrange to get the person to the nearest medical facility," Sabourin said.

Such a service can indeed be life-saving for executives and travellers who are present in regions of conflict or which are so remote that medical help is almost always out of bounds.

International SOS's New Delhi alarm centre received over 90,000 calls during the last financial year from "in trouble" foreign nationals, ranging from the trivial toothache to more serious cases.

Tanguy de Grenier de Lassagne, country general manager of International SOS, says during the 26/11 terrorist attack in Mumbai the company's alarm centre and operatives calmed not only many clients but also other foreigners stuck in the terror-hit hotels.

"We catered to not only getting our members to safety, to hospitals, but also helped a lot of foreign nationals based on specific request from their missions," said Lassagne.

Now, with the advent of the Indian transnational corporations and their expanding span, human resource managers at these conglomerates, have to make sure their senior executives are safe whichever country they travel to.

Its client roster, the officials said boasts the crème de la crème of India Inc, but declined to name them individually due to confidentiality clauses on their pacts.

"People are not very much aware of the conditions in foreign countries. With Indian companies now spreading their geographical reach, they feel the need to take care of their people who are travelling abroad," said Sabourin.

He said such services are a big hit in many countries with even governments of countries like the US, Britain and Japan, as also UN agencies, soliciting assistance for diplomats or officials travelling to places where conditions are difficult, to say the least.

"Globalisation is main driver of our success. We were not affected even by recession. In fact companies that were eearlier hesitant to expand out of home markets were forced to do so, and we are there to help in advising on local security conditions."

India, the world's largest democracy, has a very diverse population, geography and climate. India is the world's second most populous country, and the world's seventh largest country in area. Tourist facilities have varying degrees of comfort, and amenities are widely available in the major population centers and main tourist areas. Read the Department of State Background Notes on India for additional information.

REGISTRATION / EMBASSY AND CONSULATE LOCATIONS: Americans living or traveling in India are encouraged to register with the nearest U.S. Embassy or Consulate through the State Department's travel registration web and to obtain updated information on travel and security in India. Americans without Internet access may register in person with the nearest U.S. Embassy or Consulate. By registering, American citizens make it easier for the Embassy or Consulate to contact them in case of emergency.

The U.S. Embassy in New Delhi is located at Shanti Path, Chanakya Puri 110021; telephone +91-11-2419-8000; fax +91-11-2419-8407. (Note that the "+" sign indicates your international access code, which in the United States is 011-, but which is 00- in most other countries.)

The U.S. Consulate General in Mumbai (Bombay) is located at Lincoln House, 78 Bhulabhai Desai Road, 400026, telephone +91-22-2363-3611; fax +91-22-2368-5483.

The U.S. Consulate General in Kolkata (Calcutta) is at 5/1 Ho Chi Minh Sarani, 700071; telephone +91-33-3984-2400; fax +91-33-2282-2335.

The U.S. Consulate General in Chennai (Madras) is at 220 Anna Salai, Gemini Circle, 600006; telephone +91-44-2857-4000; fax +91-44-2857-4443.

The U.S. Consulate General in Hyderabad is at Paigah Palace, 1-8-323 Chiran Fort Lane, Begumpet, Secunderabad, Andhra Pradesh, 500003; telephone +91-40-4033-8300; fax +91-40-4033-8301.

ENTRY / EXIT REQUIREMENTS: U.S. citizens require a valid passport and valid Indian visa to enter and exit India for any purpose. Visitors, including those on official U.S. Government business, must obtain visas at an Indian Embassy or Consulate abroad prior to entering the country, as there are no provisions for visas upon arrival for U.S. citizens. Those arriving without a valid passport and valid visa are subject to immediate deportation. The U.S. Embassy and Consulates in India are unable to assist when U.S. citizens arrive without proper documentation. Each visitor should carry photocopies of the bio-data page of the traveler's U.S. passport and the page containing the Indian visa in order to facilitate obtaining an exit visa from the Indian government in the event of theft or loss of the passport. Replacing a lost visa, in order to exit the country, takes up to three business days.

Americans wishing to visit India are responsible for requesting the correct type of visa from the Indian Embassy or Consulate, as there generally are no provisions for changing one's immigration category (e.g., from tourist to work visa) once admitted. Tourists are generally given 6 months of legal stay upon entering India; the Government of India rarely grants extensions within the country. As of October 1, 2007, the Indian Embassy and Consulates in the U.S. outsourced the visa application process to Travisa Visa Outsourcing. Diplomatic and Official visa applications, however, are still accepted directly at the Indian Embassy and Consulates. Visitors whose primary purpose of travel is to participate in religious activities should obtain a missionary visa rather than a tourist visa. Indian immigration authorities have deported American citizens who entered India with a tourist visa and conducted religious activities. Americans who will be paid for work done while in India need employment category visas; individuals visiting India regularly on business trips including attendance at conferences should apply for a business category visa. Citizens intending to stay for an extended period of time with family, or with an unpaid NGO or volunteer activity, should apply for an entry (X) visa. Conference visas are only for designated Government of India sponsored events; all other conference attendees should get business visas. It is always best to check the Indian government website for the most up to date visa information. All U.S. government employees, including military personnel, are required to get country clearance for travel to India.

American travelers to India who work in "designated institutes and technology areas" will be subject to a two week waiting period in the visa application process and will be required to submit supplemental information with their visa application. Scholars planning to conduct research in India often need research clearances in addition to their visas. Specific information is available at the Indian Embassy and Consulates.

Foreign citizens who visit India to study, do research, work or act as missionaries, as well as all travelers planning to stay more than 180 days are required to register within 14 days of arrival with the Foreigners Regional Registration Office (FRRO) closest to where they will be staying. The FRRO maintains offices in New Delhi, Mumbai, Chennai (known as the "Chennai Immigration Office"), Kolkata and Amritsar. In other cities and small towns, the local police headquarters will normally perform this function. General information regarding Indian visa and immigration rules, including the addresses and telephone numbers for the FRRO offices, can be found at the Indian Ministry of Home Affairs website for its Bureau of Immigration. People traveling to India on a tourist visa will not be allowed reentry to India within two months unless they request specific permission from Indian Government officials in their home country. Citizens are advised to carefully review the latest regulations, which are included under the section titled "Instructions (Foreigners),"and to be aware that implementation at ports of entry may be inconsistent.

If a foreign citizen (e.g., an American) overstays his or her Indian visa, or otherwise violates Indian visa regulations, the traveler may require a clearance from the Ministry of Home Affairs in order to leave the country. Such travelers generally must pay a fine, and in some cases, may be jailed until their deportation can be arranged. Visa violators seeking an exit clearance can visit the following office any weekday from 10 a.m. - 12 noon: Ministry of Home Affairs, Foreigners Division, Jaisalmer House, 26 Man Singh Road, New Delhi 110 011 (tel. +91-11-2338-5748).

For the most current information on entry and exit requirements, please contact the Embassy of India at 2536 Massachusetts Avenue NW, Washington, DC 20008, telephone (202) 939-9806 or the Indian Consulates in Chicago, New York, San Francisco or Houston. Outside the United States, inquiries should be made at the nearest Indian embassy or consulate.

Information about dual nationality and the prevention of international child abduction can be found on our web site. (Additional information on dual nationality in India appears below under "Special Circumstances.") For further information about customs regulations, please read our Customs Information sheet.

There are no disclosure requirements or restrictions for HIV/AIDS patients who enter India on a tourist visa. Disclosure regarding HIV/AIDS is required of anyone seeking a resident permit in India. Foreign residents found to be suffering from HIV/AIDS will be deported. Please verify this information with the Embassy of India before you travel.

SAFETY AND SECURITY: Coordinated attacks in Mumbai in late November 2008 targeting areas frequented by Westerners highlighted the risk of Americans becoming intended or unintended victims of terrorism in India. There is a continuing threat from terrorism throughout India. The U.S. Government continues to receive information that terrorist groups may be planning attacks in India.

Attacks have targeted public places frequented by Westerners, including luxury and other hotels, trains, train stations, markets, cinemas, mosques, and restaurants in large urban areas. Attacks have taken place during the busy evening hours in markets and other crowded places, but could occur at any time. Some examples of recent terror attacks include the following:

" February 2010: An explosive device detonated at a café in Pune, Maharashtra, near an ashram and schools frequented by international travelers killing ten, including two foreign nationals, and injuring 50, some seriously.

" November 2008: Coordinated terrorist attacks on luxury hotels, Jewish community center, restaurant, train station, hospital and other facilities frequented by foreigners in Mumbai killed over 170, including six Americans;

" October 2008, December 2008: Multiple bombings in markets and government offices in Guwahati, Assam;

" September 2008: Five deadly explosions in New Delhi markets

" July 2008: Thirty bombs detonated in Bangalore, Karnataka and Ahmedabad, Gujarat, as well as multiple un-detonated bombs found in Surat, Gujarat;

" May 2008: A coordinated series of bombings in market and temple areas of Jaipur, Rajasthan;

Violent incidents related to local insurgencies, including those in which American citizens were injured, also occur in remote parts of India. In August 2006, two U.S. citizens were seriously injured in a grenade attack on an ISKON temple in Imphal, Manipur. Anti-Western terrorist groups, some on the U.S. Government's list of foreign terrorist organizations, are active in India, including Islamist extremist groups such as Harakat ul-Mujahidin, Jaish-e-Mohammed, Lashkar-e Tayyiba, and Harkat-ul-Jihad-i-Islami. Specific areas of concern are addressed below under "Areas of Instability."

U.S. citizens are urged to always practice good security, which includes maintaining a heightened situational awareness and a low profile. Americans are advised to monitor local news reports, vary their routes and times in carrying out daily activities, and consider the level of security present when visiting public places, including religious sites, or choosing hotels, restaurants, entertainment and recreation venues.

Beyond the threat from terrorism and insurgencies,

demonstrations often cause inconvenience. Large religious ceremonies that attract hundreds of thousands of people can result in dangerous and often life-threatening stampedes. Local demonstrations can begin spontaneously and escalate with little warning, disrupting transportation systems and city services and posing risks to travelers. In response to such events, Indian authorities occasionally impose curfews and/or restrict travel. U.S. citizens are urged to avoid demonstrations and rallies as they have the potential for violence, especially immediately preceding and following elections and religious festivals (particularly when Hindu and Muslim festivals coincide). Tensions between castes and religious groups can also result in disruptions and violence. In some cases, demonstrators specifically block roads near popular tourist sites and disrupt train operations in order to gain the attention of Indian authorities; occasionally vehicles transporting tourists are attacked in these incidents. India generally goes on "High Alert" status prior to major holidays. U.S. citizens should monitor local television and print media and contact the U.S. Embassy or the nearest U.S. Consulate for further information about the current situation in areas where they wish to travel.

Religious violence occasionally occurs in India, especially when tensions between different religious communities are purposefully exacerbated by groups pushing religiously chauvinistic agendas. Violence against Indian Christians in a remote part of Orissa in 2008 resulted in the displacement of thousands of villagers and the deaths of 40 people. There are active "anti-conversion" laws in some Indian states, and acts of conversion sometimes elicit violent reactions from Hindu extremists. Foreigners suspected of proselytizing Hindus have been attacked and killed in conservative, rural areas in India in the past.

Swimming in India: Visitors should exercise caution when swimming in open waters along the Indian coastline, particularly during the monsoon season. Every year, several people in Goa, Mumbai, Puri (Orissa), and other areas drown due to the strong undertow. It is important for visitors to heed warnings posted or advised at beaches and avoid swimming in the ocean during the monsoon season. Trained lifeguards are very rare along beaches.

Travelers to the Andaman Islands should be aware that there have been 24 reports of salt-water crocodile attacks during the past 25 years in the Islands. There have been four fatalities, including a U.S. citizen tourist in April 2010. Travelers are encouraged to seek advice from local residents about dangerous sea life before swimming and should keep a safe distance from all animals at all times.

Trekking in India: Tourists should limit trekking expeditions to routes identified for this purpose by local authorities. They should solicit assistance only from registered trekking agencies, porters and guides; suspend trekking after dark; camp at designated camping places; and ideally travel in groups of eight to ten people rather than individually or with one or two companions.

AREAS OF INSTABILITY: Jammu & Kashmir: The Department of State strongly recommends that U.S. citizens avoid travel to Jammu & Kashmir (with the exception of visits to the eastern Ladakh region and its capital, Leh) because of the potential for terrorist incidents as well as violent public unrest. A number of terrorist groups operate in the state, targeting security forces that are present throughout the region, particularly along the Line of Control (LOC) separating Indian and Pakistani-controlled Kashmir, and those stationed in the primary tourist destinations in the Kashmir Valley: Srinagar, Gulmarg, and Pahalgam.

Since 1989, as many as 60,000 people (terrorists, security forces, and civilians) have been killed in the Kashmir conflict. Many terrorist incidents take place in the state's summer capital of Srinagar, but the majority of attacks occur in rural areas. Foreigners are particularly visible, vulnerable, and definitely at risk. In the summer of 2008, serious communal violence left the state mostly paralyzed, due to massive strikes and business shut downs; several American citizens had to be evacuated. In addition, there have been attacks specifically targeted at civilians. For example: in October 2007 five soldiers and two civilians were killed in an IED blast carried out by militants in the Baramulla district of Kashmir; in August 2007 terrorists lobbed a grenade at the venue of an Independence Day function in the Bandipora district; in July 2007 a blast on an out-of-state tourist bus killed six and injured 20 civilians in the capital, Srinagar. The Indian government prohibits foreign tourists from visiting certain areas along the LOC (see the section on Restricted Areas, below). U.S. Government employees are prohibited from traveling to the state of Jammu & Kashmir (except for Ladakh) without permission, which is only granted in exceptional circumstances, from the U.S. Embassy in New Delhi. When traveling to Kashmir, U.S. official travelers attempt to lower their profiles, limit their lengths of stay, and exercise extreme caution.

India-Pakistan Border: The State Department recommends that U.S. citizens avoid travel to areas within ten kilometers of the border between India and Pakistan. Both India and Pakistan maintain a strong military presence on both sides of the border. The only official India-Pakistan border crossing point for persons who are not citizens of India or Pakistan is in the state of Punjab between Atari, India, and Wagah, Pakistan. The border crossing is usually open, but travelers are advised to confirm the current status of the border crossing prior to commencing travel. A Pakistani visa is required to enter Pakistan. An American citizen seeking a Pakistani visa while in India must first come to the U.S. Embassy in New Delhi to sign an affidavit of intent to apply for the Pakistani visa. This is a requirement of the Pakistani government.

Both India and Pakistan claim an area of the Karakoram mountain range that includes the Siachen glacier. U.S. citizens traveling to or climbing peaks in the disputed areas face significant risks. The disputed area includes the following peaks: Rimo Peak; Apsarasas I, II, and III; Tegam Kangri I, II and III; Suingri Kangri; Ghiant I and II; Indira Col; and Sia Kangri. Travelers may check with the U.S. Embassy in New Delhi for information on current conditions. (Please see the section on "Registration/Embassy and Consulate Locations" below.)

Northeast States: Incidents of violence by ethnic insurgent groups, including bombings of buses, trains, rail lines, and markets occur with a degree of frequency in parts of Assam and Manipur. While U.S. citizens have not been specifically targeted, they may be affected as bystanders. Visitors to Assam and Manipur are cautioned to avoid trains, crowds, and travel outside major cities at night. Security laws are in force, and the central government has deployed security personnel. U.S. Government employees are prohibited from traveling to the states of Assam and Manipur without permission from the U.S. Consulate in Kolkata. When traveling to these areas, U.S. official travelers attempt to lower their profiles, limit their lengths of stay, and exercise extreme caution.

Restricted Area Permits are required for foreigners to visit certain Northeastern states (see the section on Restricted Areas, below.) Travelers may check with the U.S. Consulate in Kolkata for information on current conditions. (Please see the section on Registration/Embassy and Consulate Locations, below

East, Central and Southern India: Maoist extremist groups, or "Naxalites," are active in East Central and Southern India, primarily in rural areas. Naxalites have a long history of conflict with state and national authorities, including frequent attacks on local police, paramilitary forces, and government officials and are responsible for more terrorist attacks in the country than any other organizations. Their campaign of violence and intimidation is currently on-going. Naxalites have not specifically targeted U.S. citizens but have attacked symbolic targets that have included Western companies. While Naxalite violence does not normally occur in places frequented by foreigners, there is a risk that visitors could become unintended victims due to the random nature of the indiscriminate targeting by such violent extremists.

Naxalites are active in a large swath of India from eastern Maharashtra and northern Andhra Pradhesh through western West Bengal. They are particularly active in rural parts of the Indian states of Chhattisgarh and Jharkhand and in border regions of the adjacent states of Andhra Pradesh, Maharashtra, Madhya Pradesh, Uttar Pradesh, Bihar, West Bengal and Orissa. Due to the fluid nature of the threat, the U.S. Mission requires all U.S. Government travelers to states with Naxalite activity to receive prior authorization from the Regional Security Officer responsible for the area to be visited. U.S. officials only traveling to the capital cities in these states do not need prior authorization from the Regional Security Officer.

In December 2009 and January 2010, sporadic civil unrest erupted in the south-central Indian state of Andhra Pradesh over the contentious issue of creating a separate state called Telangana within Andhra Pradesh. Until the issue is resolved definitively, there may continue to be tension, especially in the Telangana Region of Andhra Pradesh, which includes the districts of Rangareddi, Warangal, Medak, Nizamabad, Karimnagar, Adilabad, Khammam, Nalgonda, and Mahbubnagar. American citizens should avoid political rallies, demonstrations, and large crowds of any kind. The campus of Osmania University in Hyderabad has been the site of recurring civil disturbances regarding the Telangana statehood issue. U.S. citizens resident or traveling in Andhra Pradesh are reminded to monitor the situation via media sources, including TV and radio and via the Internet.

Restricted Areas: Certain parts of India are designated as "restricted areas" by the Indian Government, and require special advance permission to visit. These areas include:

" The state of Mizoram,

" The state of Manipur,

" The state of Arunachal Pradesh,

" The state of Nagaland,

" The state of Sikkim,

" Portions of the state of Himachal Pradesh near the Chinese border,

" Portions of the state of Uttarakhand (Uttaranchal) near the Chinese border,

" Portions of the state of Rajasthan near the Pakistani border,

" Portions of the state of Jammu & Kashmir near the Line of Control with Pakistan,

" The Andaman & Nicobar Islands,

" The Union Territory of the Laccadives Islands (Lakshadweep), and

" The Tibetan colony in Mundgod, Karnataka.

"Restricted Area Permits" can be obtained outside of India at Indian embassies and consulates abroad, or within India, from the Ministry of Home Affairs (Foreigners Division) at Jaisalmer House, 26 Man Singh Road, New Delhi. The states of Mizoram, Manipur, Nagaland, Arunachal Pradesh and Sikkim all maintain official guesthouses in New Delhi, each of which also can issue Restricted Area Permits for their respective states for certain travelers. Tourists also should exercise caution while visiting Mamallapuram (Mahabalipuram) in Tamil Nadu as the Indira Gandhi Atomic Research Center, Kalpakkam, is located just south of the site and is not clearly marked as a restricted and dangerous area.

For the latest security information, Americans traveling abroad should regularly monitor travel information included on the websites of the U.S. Embassy in New Delhi as well as the Consulates General in Mumbai (Bombay), Chennai (Madras), Hyderabad and Kolkata (Calcutta) (see contact information below). Americans traveling abroad should regularly monitor the Department of State, Bureau of Consular Affairs' web site, where the current Travel Warnings and Travel Alerts, as well as the Worldwide Caution, can be found.

Up-to-date information on safety and security can also be obtained by calling 1-888-407-4747 toll free in the United States and Canada or, for callers outside the United States and Canada, a regular toll-line at 1-202-501-4444. These numbers are available from 8:00 a.m. to 8:00 p.m. Eastern Time, Monday through Friday (except U.S. federal holidays).

The Department of State urges American citizens to take responsibility for their own personal security while traveling overseas. For general information about appropriate measures travelers can take to protect themselves in an overseas environment, see the Department of State's information on traveling safely abroad.

CRIME: Petty crime, especially theft of personal property, is common, particularly on trains or buses. Pickpockets can be very adept, and women have reported having their bags snatched, purse-straps cut or the bottom of their purses slit without their knowledge. Theft of U.S. passports is quite common, particularly in major tourist areas, on overnight trains, and at airports and train stations. Train travelers are urged to lock their sleeping compartments and take valuables with them when leaving their berths. Air travelers are advised to carefully watch their bags in the arrival and departure areas outside of airports. Violent crime, especially directed against foreigners, has traditionally been uncommon, although in recent years there has been a modest increase. As U.S. citizens' purchasing power is comparatively large, travelers also should exercise modesty and caution in their financial dealings in India to reduce the chance of being a target for robbery or other crime. Gangs and criminal elements operate in major cities and have sometimes targeted unsuspecting businessmen and their family members for kidnapping.

U.S. citizens, particularly women, are cautioned not to travel alone in India. Western women continue to report incidents of verbal and physical harassment by groups of men. Known in India as "Eve-teasing," these incidents can be quite frightening. While India is generally safe for foreign visitors, according to the latest figures by Indian authorities, rape is the fastest growing crime in India. Among large cities, Delhi experienced the highest number of crimes against women. Although most victims have been local residents, recent sexual attacks against female visitors in tourist areas underline the fact that foreign women are also at risk and should exercise vigilance.

Women should observe stringent security precautions, including avoiding using public transport after dark without the company of known and trustworthy companions; restricting evening entertainment to well known venues; and avoiding walking in isolated areas alone at any time of day. Female travelers are advised to respect local dress and customs. Women should also ensure their hotel room numbers remain confidential and insist the doors of their hotel rooms have chains, deadlocks, and spy-holes. In addition, it is advisable for women to hire reliable cars and drivers and avoid traveling alone in hired taxis, especially during the hours of darkness. It is preferable to obtain taxis from hotels and pre-paid taxis at airports rather than hailing them on the street. If women encounter threatening situations, they can call 100 for police assistance.

SCAMS: Major airports, train stations, popular restaurants and tourist sites are often used by scam artists looking to prey on visitors, often by creating a distraction. Taxi drivers and others, including train porters, may solicit travelers with "come-on" offers of cheap transportation and/or hotels. Travelers accepting such offers have frequently found themselves the victims of scams, including offers to assist with "necessary" transfers to the domestic airport, disproportionately expensive hotel rooms, unwanted "tours," unwelcome "purchases," and even threats to the traveler when the tourists try to decline to pay. There have been several disturbing reports of tourists being lured to and then held hostage on houseboats in Srinagar, Jammu & Kashmir, and forced to pay thousands of dollars in the face of threats of violence against the traveler and his/her family members.

Travelers should exercise care when hiring transportation and/or guides and use only well-known travel agents to book trips. Some scam artists have lured travelers by displaying their name on a sign when they leave the airport. Another popular scam is to drop money or to squirt something on the clothing of an unsuspecting traveler and during the distraction to rob them of their valuables. Individual tourists have also been given drugged drinks or tainted food to make them more vulnerable to theft, particularly at train stations. Even food or drink purchased in front of the traveler from a canteen or vendor could be tainted. To protect against robbery of personal belongings, it is best not to accept food or drink from strangers.

Some vendors sell carpets, jewelry, gemstones or other expensive items that may not be of the quality promised. Travelers should deal only with reputable businesses and should not hand over credit cards or money unless they are certain that goods being shipped to them are the goods they purchased. If a deal sounds too good to be true, it is best avoided. Most Indian states have official tourism bureaus set up to handle travelers' complaints.

Travelers should be aware of a number of other scams that have been perpetrated against foreign travelers, particularly in Goa, Jaipur, and Agra. The scams generally target younger travelers and involve suggestions that money can be made by privately transporting gems or gold (both of which can result in arrest) or by taking delivery abroad of expensive carpets, supposedly while avoiding customs duties. The scam artists describe profits that can be made upon delivery of the goods, and require the traveler to pay a "deposit" as part of the transaction.

INFORMATION FOR VICTIMS OF CRIME: If you are the victim of a crime while overseas, in addition to reporting to local police, please contact the nearest U.S. Embassy or Consulate for assistance. The Embassy/Consulate staff can, for example, assist you to find appropriate medical care, contact family members or friends and explain how funds could be transferred. Although the investigation and prosecution of the crime is solely the responsibility of local authorities, consular officers can help you to understand the local criminal justice process and to find an attorney if needed. Victims of a crime in India should obtain a copy of the police report (called an "FIR" or "First Information Report") from local police at the time of reporting the incident. A copy of this report is helpful for insurance purposes in replacing lost valuables. Local authorities generally are unable to take any meaningful action without the filing of a police report.

The loss or theft abroad of a U.S. passport should be reported immediately to the local police and the nearest U.S. Embassy or Consulate. An FIR is required by the Indian Government in order to obtain an exit visa to leave India in the event of a lost or stolen passport. Although the Embassy or Consulate is able to replace a stolen or lost passport the Ministry of Home Affairs and the Foreigners Regional Registration Office (FRRO) are responsible for approving an exit visa. This process generally takes two to three business days.

The local equivalent to the "911" emergency line in India is "100." An additional emergency number, "112," can be accessed from mobile phones.

CRIMINAL PENALTIES: While in a foreign country, a U.S. citizen is subject to that country's laws and regulations, which sometimes differ significantly from those in the United States and may not afford the protections available to the individual under U.S. law. Penalties for breaking the law can be more severe than in the United States for similar offenses. Persons violating Indian laws, even unknowingly, may be expelled, arrested or imprisoned. For example, certain comments or gestures towards women, Indian national symbols, or religion that are legal in the United States may be considered a criminal violation in India, subjecting the accused to possible fines or imprisonment. Furthermore, since the police may arrest anyone who is accused of committing a crime (even if the allegation is frivolous in nature), the Indian criminal justice system is often used to escalate personal disagreements into criminal charges. This practice has been increasingly exploited by dissatisfied business partners, contractors, estranged spouses, or other persons with whom the U.S. citizen has a disagreement, occasionally resulting in the jailing of U.S. citizens pending resolution of their disputes. At the very least, such circumstances can delay the U.S. citizen's timely departure from India, and may result in an unintended long-term stay in the country. Corruption in India, especially at local levels, is a concern, as evidenced by Transparency International's Corruption Perception Index of 2008, ranking India in 85th place among the world's 180 countries. Penalties for possession, use, or trafficking in illegal drugs in India are severe, and convicted offenders can expect long jail sentences and heavy fines. Engaging in sexual conduct with children or using or disseminating child pornography in a foreign country is a crime, prosecutable in the United States.

American citizens arrested in India have a right to notify, or have officials notify, the nearest Embassy or Consulate upon arrest. Though the Embassy and Consulates may not intervene in legal matters they can provide information on lawyers, the local justice system, can visit the incarcerated person on a regular basis, and can serve as a liaison with parties approved by the incarcerated individual.

Special Circumstances

Dual Nationality: In 2006, India launched the "Overseas Citizens of India" (OCI) program, which has often been mischaracterized as a dual nationality program, as it does not grant Indian citizenship. Thus, an American who obtains an OCI card is not a citizen of India and remains a citizen of the United States. An OCI card in reality is similar to a U.S. "green card" in that a holder can travel to and from India indefinitely, work in India, study in India, and own property in India (except for certain agricultural and plantation properties). An OCI holder, however, does not receive an Indian passport, cannot vote in Indian elections and is not eligible for Indian government employment. The OCI program is similar to the Persons of Indian Origin (PIO) card introduced by the Indian government several years ago, except that PIO holders must still register with Indian immigration authorities, and PIO cards are not issued for an indefinite period. American citizens of Indian descent can apply for PIO or OCI cards at the Indian Embassy in Washington, or at the Indian Consulates in Chicago, New York, San Francisco and Houston. Inside India, American citizens can apply at the nearest FRRO office (please see "Entry/Exit Requirements" section above for more information on the FRRO).

Religious Activities: Foreign visitors planning to engage in religious proselytizing are required by Indian law to have a "missionary" visa. Immigration authorities have determined that certain activities, including speaking at religious meetings to which the general public is invited, may violate immigration law if the traveler does not hold a missionary visa. Foreigners with tourist visas who engage in missionary activity are subject to deportation and possible criminal prosecution. The states of Orissa, Chhattisgarh, Gujarat, Himachal Pradesh, and Madhya Pradesh have active "anticonversion" legislation regulating conversion from one religious faith to another. Arunachal Pradesh currently has an inactive "anticonversion" law awaiting accompanying regulations needed for enforcement. U.S. citizens intending to engage in missionary activity may wish to seek legal advice to determine whether the activities they intend to pursue are permitted under Indian law.

Customs Restrictions: Indian customs authorities enforce strict regulations concerning temporary importation into or export from India of items such as firearms, ammunition, antiquities, electronic equipment, currency, ivory, gold objects, and other prohibited materials. Even transit passengers require permission from the Government of India to bring in such items. Those not complying risk arrest and/or fine and confiscation of these items. If charged with any alleged legal violations by Indian law enforcement, it is recommended that an attorney review any document prior to signing. The Government of India requires the registration of antique items with the local police along with a photograph of the item. It is advisable to contact the Embassy of India in Washington or one of India's consulates in the United States for specific information regarding customs requirements. More information is available from the Indian Central Board of Excise and Customs. Another useful site is the Indira Gandhi International Airport Office of the Joint Commissioner of Customs . In many countries around the world, including India, counterfeit and pirated goods are widely available. Transactions involving such products may be illegal under Indian law. In addition, bringing them back to the United States may result in forfeitures and/or fines. More information on this serious problem is available in a report prepared by the Office of the United States Trade Representative called the Special 301 Report. This report is updated each year.

Indian customs authorities encourage the use of an ATA (Admission Temporaire/Temporary Admission) Carnet for the temporary admission of professional equipment, commercial samples, and/or goods for exhibitions and fair purposes. ATA Carnet Headquarters, located at the U.S. Council for International Business, 1212 Avenue of the Americas, New York, NY 10036, issues and guarantees the ATA Carnet in the United States. For additional information call (212) 354-4480, or emai USCIB for details. Please see our Customs Information.

Natural Disaster Threats: Parts of northern India are highly susceptible to earthquakes. Regions of highest risk, ranked 5 on a scale of 1 to 5, include areas around Srinagar, Himachal Pradesh, Rishikesh and Dehra Dun, the northern parts of Punjab, northwest Gujarat, northern Bihar, and the entire northeast. Ranked 4 (high damage risk) is an area that sweeps along the north through Jammu and Kashmir, Eastern Punjab, Haryana, Northern Uttar Pradesh, central Bihar and the northern parts of West Bengal. New Delhi is located in zone 4. Severe flooding is common in Bihar, Assam and Orissa.

MEDICAL FACILITIES AND HEALTH INFORMATION: The quality of medical care in India varies considerably. Medical care is available in the major population centers that approaches and occasionally meets Western standards, but adequate medical care is usually very limited or unavailable in rural areas. .

Indian health regulations require all travelers arriving from Sub-Saharan Africa or other yellow-fever areas to have evidence of vaccination against yellow fever. Travelers who do not have such proof are subject to immediate deportation or a six-day detention in the yellow-fever quarantine center. U.S. citizens, who transit through any part of sub-Saharan Africa, even for one day, are advised to carry proof of yellow fever immunization.

Information on vaccinations and other health precautions, such as safe food and water precautions and insect-bite protection, may be obtained from the Centers for Disease Control and Prevention's hotline for international travelers at 1-877-FYI-TRIP (1-877-394-8747) or via the CDC's web site. For information about outbreaks of infectious diseases abroad consult the World Health Organization's (WHO) web site. These websites provide useful information, such as suggested vaccinations for visitors to India, safe food and water precautions, appropriate measures to avoid contraction of mosquito-borne diseases (such as malaria and Japanese B encephalitis), suggestions to avoid altitude sickness, etc. Further, these sites provide information on disease outbreaks that may arise from time to time - outbreaks of mosquito-borne viral diseases such as dengue fever and chikungunya occur in various parts of India each year, so travelers should check the sites shortly before traveling to India. Further health information for travelers is available from the WHO.

Outbreaks of Avian Influenza (H5N1 virus) occur intermittently in eastern India, including West Bengal, Manipur, Sikkim and Assam. There have been no reported cases of Avian Influenza infections in human beings. Updates on the avian influenza situation in India are published on the Embassy's web site. For further information on avian influenza (bird flu), please refer to the Department of State's Avian Influenza Fact Sheet.

H1N1, also known as the swine flu, has been reported in India in travelers coming from or transiting through the U.S. Individuals traveling with flu like symptoms should strongly consider delaying their travel until their symptoms have resolved for the protection of other passengers and the risk of being quarantined in a communicable public hospital on arrival in India. H1N1 vaccine is not available in India; seasonal influenza vaccine is available. H1N1 influenza is currently found and has spread locally throughout India.

Tuberculosis is an increasingly serious health concern in India. For further information, please consult the CDC's Travel Notice on TB.

Medical tourism is a rapidly growing industry. Companies offering vacation packages bundled with medical consultations and financing options provide direct-to-consumer advertising over the internet. Such medical packages often claim to provide high quality care, but the quality of health care in India is highly variable. People seeking health care in India should understand that medical systems operate differently from those in the United States and are not subject to the same rules and regulations. Anyone interested in traveling for medical purposes should consult with their local physician before traveling and refer to the information from CDC.

The Supreme Court recently sanctioned commercial surrogacy in India and is currently debating an Assisted Reproductive Technology (ART) Bill that will establish national guidelines for institutions and clients. India is also formulating a policy to investigate all foreign surrogacy cases at the time of departure, a process that could last up to one month after the birth of the child.

Anyone considering traveling to India for ART procedures should contact the Embassy or one of the Consulates for updated U.S. Government requirements.

The U.S. Embassy and Consulates in India maintain lists of local doctors and hospitals, all of which are published on their respective websites under "U.S. Citizen Services." Please see "Embassy and Consulate Locations" section below.

MEDICAL INSURANCE: The Department of State strongly urges Americans to consult with their medical insurance company prior to traveling abroad to confirm whether their policy applies overseas and whether it will cover emergency expenses such as a medical evacuation. Insurers rarely make payment directly to overseas healthcare providers. For heath care received in India, you will most likely need to pay up front and be reimbursed later for expenses you incur during treatment. Please see our information on medical insurance overseas.

TRAFFIC SAFETY AND ROAD CONDITIONS: While in a foreign country, U.S. citizens may encounter road conditions that differ significantly from those in the United States. The information below concerning India is provided for general reference only, and may not be totally accurate in a particular location or circumstance.

Travel by road in India is dangerous. A number of U.S. citizens have suffered fatal traffic accidents in recent years. Travel at night is particularly hazardous. Buses, patronized by hundreds of millions of Indians, are convenient in that they serve almost every city of any size. However, they are usually driven fast, recklessly, and without consideration for the rules of the road. Accidents are quite common. Trains are safer than buses, but train accidents still occur more frequently than in developed countries.

In order to drive in India, one must have either a valid Indian driver's license or a valid international driver's license. Because of difficult road and traffic conditions, many Americans who visit India choose to hire a local driver.

On Indian roads, the safest driving policy is to always assume that other drivers will not respond to a traffic situation in the same way you would in the United States. On Indian roads, might makes right, and buses and trucks epitomize this fact. For instance, buses and trucks often run red lights and merge directly into traffic at yield points and traffic circles. Cars, auto-rickshaws, bicycles and pedestrians behave only slightly more cautiously. Frequent use of one's horn or flashing of headlights to announce one's presence is both customary and wise.

Outside major cities, main roads and other roads are often poorly maintained and congested. Even main roads frequently have only two lanes, with poor visibility and inadequate warning markers. On the few divided highways one can expect to meet local transportation traveling in the wrong direction, often without lights. Heavy traffic is the norm and includes (but is not limited to) overloaded trucks and buses, scooters, pedestrians, bullock and camel carts, horse or elephant riders en route to weddings, bicycles, and free-roaming livestock. Traffic in India moves on the left. It is important to be alert while crossing streets and intersections, especially after dark as traffic is coming in the "wrong" direction (i.e., from the left). Travelers should remember to use seatbelts in both rear and front seats where available, and to ask their drivers to maintain a safe speed.

If a driver hits a pedestrian or a cow, the vehicle and its occupants are at risk of being attacked by passersby. Such attacks pose significant risk of injury or death to the vehicle's occupants or at least of incineration of the vehicle. It can thus be unsafe to remain at the scene of an accident of this nature, and drivers may instead wish to seek out the nearest police station.

Protestors often use road blockage as a means of publicizing their grievances, causing severe inconvenience to travelers. Visitors should monitor local news reports for any reports of road disturbances.

Emergency Numbers: The following emergency numbers work in New Delhi, Mumbai, Chennai, Hyderabad and Kolkata:

" Police 100

" Fire Brigade 101

" Ambulance 102

AVIATION SAFETY OVERSIGHT: The U.S. Federal Aviation Administration (FAA) has assessed the Government of India's Civil Aviation Authority as being in compliance with International Civil Aviation Organization (ICAO) aviation safety standards for oversight of India's air carrier operations. For more information, travelers may visit the FAA's web site.

CHILDREN'S ISSUES: India is not a signatory to the Hague Convention on the Civil Aspects of International Parental Child Abduction (although the Government of India has expressed its intention to sign the convention at some point in the future), nor is the abduction of one's own child considered to be a crime under Indian law. For information see our Office of Children's Issues web pages on intercountry adoption and international parental child abduction. See our web site for abduction information specific to India.

This replaces the Country Specific Information for India dated July 9, 2009, to update the sections on Registration/Embassy and Consulate Locations , Entry/Exit Requirements, Threats to Safety and Security, Areas of Instability, Crime, Victims of Crime, Criminal Penalties, Special Circumstances, Medical Facilities and Health Information, and Aviation Safety Oversight.

Charles Landry, Urban Consultant

Landry is recognized as an international authority on creativity and cities' futures. Through his company, Comedia, established in 1978, he has assisted dozens of countries, from the wealthy to the underdeveloped, in balancing the concerns of urban development with tradition, culture, and creativity. His focus is on finding ways for culture to invigorate and enhance economies. Landry works closely with local leaders to inspire, facilitate, and stimulate ideas that transform cities. He has found original solutions to seemingly intractable urban problems such as marrying innovation and tradition, balancing wealth creation and social cohesiveness, and preserving local character while focusing on a global orientation.

Crispin Raymond, Creative Tourism Consultant

Raymond has a 25 year background in the arts, first as chief executive of the Theater Royal in Bath, England, and subsequently as the founder and leader of a consulting firm specializing in policy, management, building, and funding issues for charitable and arts organizations. Raymond and Greg Richards coined the term "creative tourism" and launched Creative Tourism New Zealand in 2003.

Greg Richards, Tourism Consultant

A partner in the company Tourism Research and Marketing, Richards has worked with many governments. He has extensive experience in tourism research and has held positions at universities in Spain, the Netherlands, and England. He is also the author of well-known publications on creative and cultural tourism and is a co-founder of Creative Tourism New Zealand along with Crispin Raymond. As a European executive member of the Association for Tourism and Leisure Education (ATLAS), he has directed projects on topics including cultural tourism, crafts tourism, sustainable tourism, tourism education, and labor mobility in the tourism industry. He has worked extensively on developing creative tourism in Barcelona and Burgos, Spain; Manchester, Newcastle, London, and Edinburgh, United Kingdom; Amsterdam, Rotterdam and Den Bosch, Netherlands; Sibiu, Romania; Amman, Jordan; and Macao, China. He is currently working with the Dutch city of Den Bosch to develop a series of events celebrating the 500th anniversary of painter Heironymus Bosch.

Hayes Lewis, Center for Life Long Education, Institute of American Indian Arts

Hayes Lewis is the Director of the Center for Lifelong Education (CLE) at the Institute of American Indian Arts (IAIA).

Zuni Pueblo tribal member. The Center for Lifelong Education (CLE) is the newest organizational development within IAIA and represents the tribal outreach, technical services, extended education and cultural exchange component of the institute. The CLE provides a multi-faceted range of high quality outreach education, training, technical assistance and capacity development opportunities for Indigenous people and tribes. Organizational & programming priorities designed to strengthen IAIA-CLE services include: educational extension and tribal outreach, partnership development, international cultural exchanges and collaboration with the Center for Arts and Cultural Studies (CACS) and the IAIA Museum to sponsor exceptional learning opportunities for the students and community.

Jay Walljasper, Writer, Editor, Consultant, Speaker

Walljasper is presently a contributing editor to National Geographic Traveler magazine, as well as the executive editor of Ode, a magazine about news and culture published in the Netherlands, and a senior fellow at New York's Project for Public Spaces. Previously, he held editorial positions for Utne and Utne Reader. He has contributed stories to important publications all over the world and has written and edited several books, most recently, The Great Neighborhood Book, a guide to fixing broken neighborhoods and how citizens can save the world on their own block. Walljasper focuses on urban issues, searching for inspiring developments and ideas around the world.

Eric Maisel, Creative Coach and Author

Maisel has been coaching performing and creative artists for more than twenty years. He trains other creative coaches and has written more than thirty books, including Coaching the Artist Within, Fearless Creating, A Writer's Paris, A Writer's San Francisco, The Van Gogh Blues, The Creativity Book, Performance Anxiety, Ten Zen Seconds, and others. He has also written for many magazines and is a well-known speaker on creativity issues and coaching. He holds masters degrees in counseling and creative writing and a doctorate in counseling psychology.

Alex Pattakos, Ph.D., Author

Alex Pattakos, Ph.D., affectionately nicknamed "Dr. Meaning," is the founder of the Center for Meaning and author of the international best-selling book, Prisoners of Our Thoughts: Viktor Frankl's Principles for Discovering Meaning in Life and Work .He is a former therapist and mental health administrator, political campaign organizer, and full-time university professor (and graduate program head) of public and business administration. He has worked closely with several Presidential administrations on social and economic policy matters, and served as an adviser to the Commissioner of the U.S. Food and Drug Administration. Dr. Pattakos was also one of the initial faculty evaluators for the Innovations In American Government Awards Program at the John F. Kennedy School of Government, Harvard University, and has been a faculty member at The Brookings Institution. He has published extensively in the peer-reviewed political science and public administration literatures, and is the co-author of the book, From Nation to States: The Small Cities Community Development Block Grant Program, published by the State University of New York (SUNY Press). A former member of the elected National Council of the American Society for Public Administration (ASPA), Alex also is a past president of Renaissance Business Associates (RBA), an international, nonprofit association of people committed to elevating the human spirit in the workplace. During his tenure as President, RBA was active in Australia, Canada, Europe, Nigeria, South Africa, and the USA. Dr. Pattakos understands the challenges facing people in today's uncertain times. Through his work with Fortune 500 companies, public and nonprofit organizations, and university teaching, Alex has helped people at all levels and in all walks of life build their capacities for personal and organizational transformation. Moreover, as a principal of The Innovation Group (www.seedsofinnovation.com), he consults internationally with individuals, teams, and organizations in all sectors and industries with an explicit focus on designing innovation systems, processes, products, and policies that make a positive difference and that are truly "meaningful."

Rebecca Anderson, Executive Director of HandMade in America

HandMade in America is a pioneering organization located in Ashville, North Carolina. It promotes economic development, sustainability, and heritage tourism through its support for handmade objects. As executive director, Anderson oversees operations that involve 3,000 citizens and 20 regional partnerships. She also serves as a consultant for cultural and economic development programs related to crafts. Previously, she was director of economic development for the Ashville Chamber of Commerce. She has held several positions in community and economic development and helped establish the first federal day care program in the region. She was named one of "America's Top Twenty Visionaries" by U.S. News and World Report in 1999.

Geoffrey Godbey, Professor Emeritus at Pennsylvania State University

Dr. Godbey is the president of Next Consulting, a company dedicated to the re-positioning of leisure and tourism services for the future, and Professor Emeritus in the department of Recreation, Parks, and Tourism Management at Pennsylvania State University. He has written 10 books and more than 100 articles about leisure, time use, work, aging, recreation, health, parks, and the future. He is past president of the Academy of Leisure Sciences. He has also appeared on television and has written for a number of popular magazines. He has donc research and consulting for many clients, including AARP, the U.S. Forest Service, the U.S. Department of Interior, the government of Sao Paulo, Brazil, the National Recreation Foundation, and the National Science Foundation. He has advised numerous advertising agencies and recreation, park, and tourism organizations. A frequent speaker, Godbey has given presentations in twenty- four countries.

ROBERT MCNULTY, FOUNDER AND PRESIDENT OF PARTNERS FOR LIVABLE COMMUNITIES

Partners for Livable Communities, a twenty-year-old non-profit organization, is a national leader on issues of livability in American cities. Partners utilizes a number of pathways-advocacy, information, leadership, and guidance-to help communities solve their problems. As the founder and head of the organization, McNulty is known for his ability to forge effective public-private partnerships that can transform cities. Prior to founding Partners, McNulty had a distinguished career in federal agencies and as a professor at the Columbia University School of Architecture. He is a frequent writer, editor, and lecturer on urban issues. He holds an undergraduate degree in business, a law degree, and was a Loeb Fellow at the Harvard Graduate School of Design.

L. KELLEY LINDQUIST, PRESIDENT, ARTSPACE PROJECTS

Artspace, a non-profit organization, is the nation's leader in developing space for artists. Under Lindquist's leadership, Artspace has completed 18 major projects with a total value of more than $175 million. This includes 14 live/work projects with more than 560 units. Artspace has won numerous awards, including the National Trust for Historic Preservation's Honor Award for contributing to the revitalization of inner-city communities. The St. Paul Company's Leadership in Neighborhoods Award allowed him to study government supported housing for artists in Great Britain, Austria, Germany, and the former Soviet Union. He is in demand as a speaker and consultant and increasingly focuses on larger issues concerning the role of arts in American society.

JACK LOEFFLER, HISTORIAN, WRITER, RADIO PRODUCER, AND SOUND COLLAGE ARTIST

Loeffler has produced nearly 300 radio programs, including the thirteen part series, The Spirit of Place and the 6 part series, Moving Waters: The Colorado River and the West. His books include Adventures with Ed: A Portrait of Abbey, La Musica de los

Veijitos: The Hispanic Folk Music of the Rio Grande del Norte, and Interviews with Iconoclasts. He is currently on a 4 year grant from the Ford Foundation to document the relationships of indigenous cultures to their habitats, a project that will result in a radio series and a book. Loeffler is an advocate of grass roots activism in reshaping communities' futures.

Kalyan sengupta, Assistant Director, India tourism, joined his post in New york two years ago. A quite and unassuming man, he has tirelessly promoted India as a tourism destination in the us since he arrived here from Delhi where he had been posted earlier. in the following interview to NRI Today, mr. sengupta, who joined the ministry of tourism 25 years ago, spoke about the challenges he has faced in the course of his work here and the future of tourism in India.

My term in usA was one of the most exciting & challenging one. usA is the largest source market for tourists for India. thus working in usA has always been a challenge. During my tenure at India tourism, New york, the first ever mega Event in North America - a series of events to showcase India in various parts of New york was staged over a period of three days; then a big delegation of tour operators from India came and a series of road shows with major buyers and the local media was arranged. Besides, there were many other events arranged in the usA and south America. .

The us market is one of the most challenging one. American travelers are very much value conscious. thus we are required to deliver what we promise. As India has so much of variety there are products for every type of tourists. thus it is not difficult to satisfy American tourists.

India's culture is a unique blend of old and new, tradition and technology. A trip to India offers a delightful glimpse into its exotic culture shaped by religion, history, and artistry. From temples to forts and mausoleums, India offers a plethora of architectural attractions - the incomparable taj mahal, rightfully described by Nobel Laureate poet rabindranath tagore as "a teardrop on the cheek of time;" the well preserved pink sandstone Agra Fort;

Fatehpur sikri, a monument to Indian structural design; the erotic sculptures of Khajuraho; the breathtaking craftsmanship of the magnificent Ellora and Buddhist & Jain paintings in Ajanta carved into a mountainside in maharashtra between 600 and 1000 AD, just to name a few.

For nature lovers, we have our rich and diverse wildlife preserved in the 80 national parks, 441 sanctuaries and 23 tiger reserves. For Wildlife enthusiasts, India is the perfect place to see wild animals in their natural habitat. the tea gardens of Darjeeling and the mughal gardens in Kashmir are some of the finest in the country, with beautiful native flowers, various lush trees bordering lakes and manmade water channels. Added to this are the many beaches, deltas, deserts, many luxurious hotels and resorts, picturesque nature sites, and its exotic and varied cuisine that make India a mecca for tourists.

We promoted India in the us market as a safe destination full of variety & as a lifetime experience. the visit to India is for self discovery, self fulfillment & self realization. in addition, we have many new products like Wellness tourism, medical tourism, various kinds of Adventure tourism, miCE tourism, Cruise tourism, etc. however, Cultural tourism still remains as the backbone of our tourism promotion. our promotion with

"Incredible India" branding tries to position India as a unique destination & truly incredible! "incredible India" branding for tourism promotion is one of the most successful brand campaign of the world. Even it got the attention of several us Congressman who referred this brand campaign as an example which may be tried for promotion of tourism in usA. thus incredible India campaign has boosted hugely to promote India as a tourist destination. in fact, the campaign bagged the prestigious Grand Prix Award CiFFt (the international Committee of tourism Film Festivals) in Vienna, Austria recently.

We do not have any figures for 2009. however, in 2008, the us was the No.1 country as the source market for tourists to India. in 2008, about one million American tourists visited India. mumbai terrorist attack is an act by some outside terrorist groups. this type of incident can happen in any parts of the world and can be compared to the 9/11 tragedy in New york. Global terrorism has affected many countries, including India. the Indian government's prime concern is the security and safety of tourists and it has taken various steps in that regard. under the directions of the ministry of tourism, various state governments have introduced special police squads to protect tourists. here in New york, we arranged an event for the tour operators and media at the Consulate General of India in Ny after the mumbai terrorist attacks, where Consul General Prabhu Dayal assured all the tour operators and media about the steps being taken for the safety and security of tourists visiting India.

The ministry of tourism has evolved various kinds of new tourist products to boost the tourist traffic to India. As mentioned earlier we are promoting Wellness tourism, medical tourism, miCE tourism, Cruise tourism, various kinds of adventure tourism, rural tourism, etc.

India tourism, New york, will continue its promotion of tourism with incredible India Branding in 2010 also. it will try to Position India as a unique tourist destination; Promote India as a global brand to take advantage of the burgeoning global travel trade and its vast untapped potential as a destination; Promote India as a safe and affordable destination; and, ensure that the tourist gets physically invigorated, mentally rejuvenated, culturally enriched, spiritually elevated and "feel India from within."

Until now, the Golden triangle - Delhi- Agra - Jaipur is the most popular with American tourists. But there other places in India's eastern and southern parts that require to be promoted more and need more attention and we are currently in the process of bringing those areas to the notice of international tourists.

Your message to the readers!

The visit to India is once in a lifetime experience. in India tourists are regarded as God. We call in sanskrit "Atithi Debo Bhavo." thus we like to invite everybody to visit our India, which is truly incredible.

Iran Safety and Security For Tourists

Iran is very safe and people will be prepared to help you in any difficulty - it would be a matter of national pride.

Theft is rare and even the secret police leave tourists alone. Still, it's best for guys not to try and talk to women in the street.

The water is clean and the food is safe.

If you meet someone who gets fundamental on you or tries to argue about politics don't waste your breath. As in any Muslim country you can silence any nuisance by asking:

'Why are you talking to me like this? Am I not a guest in your country?"

He will then be too ashamed to continue.

The traffic is outrageous in some places. I actually had to have someone play boy scout and help me cross the road.

Your main danger is indigestion if you're invited to stay with a family. Food never stops coming from the kitchen all day and it's a point of honor to eat. Iranian mothers sometimes break down crying if their guests don't eat enough.

Stay Safe

In general Iran is much safer than many from the West might believe. Most people are genuinely friendly and interested to know about you and your country, so leave aside your preconceptions and come with an open mind. Iran is still a relatively low-crime country, although thefts and muggings have been on the increase in recent years. Keep your wits about you, and take the usual precautions against pickpockets in crowded bazaars and buses.

In particular, the tourist center of Isfahan has had problems with muggings of foreigners in unlicensed taxis, and fake police making random checks of tourists' passports. Only use official taxis, and never allow 'officials' to make impromptu searches of your belongings.

Try not to travel in the southeastern area of Iran, meaning the provinces of Sistan and Baluchistan, and also to some degree

Southern Khorasan province. Drug trade is very common with smuggling from Afghanistan and other crimes as robbery, killing and kidnapping. Some cities as Zahedan, Zabol and Mirjaveh are particularly dangerous but that doesn't mean that every place in this area of Iran is dangerous, Chahbahar which is close to the Pakistani border is a very calm and friendly city.

Women travellers should not encounter any major problems when visiting Iran, but will undoubtedly be the subject of at least some unwanted attention. Perceptions of Western women among local men, fuelled largely by satellite television and Baywatch reruns, have led to the assumption that all foreign women like to dress and act like Pamela Anderson. A stern look should be enough to deter amorous locals.

Gay and lesbian travelers should err on the side of discretion in Iran. Under the strict Sharia law, sodomy is punishable by death and lesbian sex is punishable with lashes, though this law only applies to Iranian citizens and those who engage in such activities with Iranian citizens. While public displays of platonic affection between members of the same sex -- such as holding hands, arms draped over shoulders and kissing on the cheek -- are not uncommon, foreign visitors who are gay or lesbian probably should be very discreet considering the possibility of harassment by security forces. The vast majority of Iranians have unfavourable views of same-sex relationships, but this rarely manifests in personal, violent attacks against homosexuals. In the event that a gay or lesbian visitor is somehow "outed," they can be expected to be immediately deported.

Watch out for joobs (???), the open storm water drains that shoulder every road and are easy to miss when walking in the dark.

Ignore the media hype, your chances of facing anti-Western sentiment as a traveller are slim. Even hardline Iranians make a clear distinction between the Western governments they distrust and individual travelers who visit their country. Americans may receive the odd jibe about their government's policies, but usually nothing more serious than that. However, it is always best to err on the side of caution and avoid politically-oriented conversations, particularly in taxi cabs. In addition, a few Iranian-Americans have been detained recently and accused of espionage. These kind of incidents are rare, but still the broader implications are worth considering and bearing in mind

Iranian traffic is horrendous. Drivers attack their art with an equal mix of aggressiveness and incompetence and view road rules here do not exist! Guidelines are lax and rarely followed. Take care when crossing the roads, and even greater care when driving on them - Iranian drivers tend to overtake along pavements and any section of the road where there is space.

There are a lot of military and other sensitive facilities in Iran. Photography near military and other government installations is strictly prohibited. Any transgression may result in detention and serious criminal charges, including espionage, which can carry the death penalty. Do not photograph any military object, jails, harbours, or telecommunication devices, airports or other objects and facilities which you suspect are military in nature. Be aware that this rule is taken very seriously in Iran.

Emergencies

Emergency services are extensive in Iran, and response times are very good compared to other local regions, 110 is the telephone number of the local Police control center, it is probably easiest to phone 110, as the local police have direct contact with other emergency services, and will probably be the only number with English speaking operators.Other Emergency Services are also available via 115 for Ambulances and 125 for the Fire and Rescue team (these numbers are frequently answered by the Ambulance or Fire crew operating from them, there is little guarantee these men will speak English). The international number 112 is available from cell phones, and will usually connect you to the Police. Iran has also "Iran Assistance" an insurance company specializing in international medical evacuation.

Stay healthy

Iran has state-of-the-art medical facilities in all its major cities. Apart from being up to date with your usual travel vaccinations (tetanus, polio, etc) no special preparation is needed for travel to Iran.

Tap water is safe to drink in most of the country (and especially the cities), although you may find the chalkiness and taste off-putting in some areas (mainly Qom, Yazd, Hormozgan and Boushehr provinces). Bottled mineral water (?b ma'dani) is widely available. Also, on many streets and sites, public water fridges are installed to provide drinking water.

Respect

In general, Iranians are warm, friendly and generous individuals with a strong interest in foreigners and other cultures. In dealing with Iranians, the following tips relating to customs and etiquette may prove useful:

The liberalisation in Iran is going backward and the legally-enforced Islamic codes of conduct dictate many aspects of public life. Respecting the dozens of unspoken rules and regulations of Iranian life can be a daunting prospect for travellers, but don't be intimidated. As a foreigner you will be given leeway and it doesn't take long to acclimatise yourself. Moreover, some limitations that are quite disgusting for the people forced to abide can be fun for the unaccuctomed foreign tourist who is assured to go back to the normal conditions after the stay.

Top Safety Tips for Women Travelers

It's a fact that women need to travel with a little special care; horror stories do exist and women, taught to have a care in life in general, can toss cares to the wind on vacation (like all travelers can) and lose that finely tuned caution edge that they keep honed on their own city streets.

Don't let concerns stop you, though - just remember to follow the same basic street rules you would at home (or learn them)...

and, in the words of veteran female traveler Zahara Heckscher, "Stay safe but don't stay home!".

AVOIDING TRAVEL THEFT

Thieves often perceive females as easier targets for theft than men. After all, aren't they the weaker sex? (Not!) The most obvious solution is sticking to the safer parts of town, but you'll certainly miss adventure if you do.

Carry a light

Consider avoiding deserted streets after dark; if you can't, then carry a small, heavy flashlight in your hand. Be careful on dark streets even if you have a companion.

Watch the crowd

Some thieves prefer crowded areas - stay alert in places like bus stations and during street celebrations, where you're likely to be jostled -- thieves use these circumstances to grab your stuff.

Consider your undies

Muggers aren't interested in your bra. Sew pockets into it where you can keep some folded cash; if you do get mugged, you're not left helpless. A money belt works, too, but thieves know all about money belts (and would you really use one at home, or on the streets of New York or Chicago?). I also sometimes stash a couple of bigger bills in a sock after dark or anytime in some places, since I can be the world's most careless person about cash in pockets.

Don't bring the bling

Avoid ostentatious jewelry; you could be injured if a thief yanks a bracelet from your wrist or a necklace from your throat.

Let the bag go

Most experts say not to resist -- let your bag go and then shout for help rather than risk assault. Opening your wallet and handing over your money may be enough for the thief and you can keep your bag -- it also may make a thief think you're reaching for a weapon. Better to hand over the bag.

Consider Your Attire

Dressing well can make a thief think you have mounds of moolah in your bag. And women's dress can be a major issue in some developing countries. Remember that, until recently, Afghanistan women had to cover themselves from head to toe or risk legal repercussions. It's already pretty clear that you're a Westerner -- avoid looking like a rich Westerner to avoid creepy kinds of attention.

Dress like a local

Learn the local dress code as soon as you arrive; buy appropriate clothing locally if neccesary. In some countries, typical American young women's attire like a shirt that shows your belly may be an offensive slap in the face to local women and an invitation for a come-on from the men. In Islamic countries, lay aside your own opinions and wear a head scarf - read more about clothing in Muslim countries.

Avoid Unwanted Guy Attention

You're young, you're on an adventure, and you may want some attention from that guy you've just met. Just don't invite him back to your hotel room until you know he's a safe guy -- and remember that what you think is not okay may not be clear if you don't speak the language.

Follow these tips to avoid unwanted attention.

The oldest trick

Consider buying a cheap wedding ring, even if you're a teenager. Especially in developing countries, a married woman is viewed as the property of another man and therefore off limits. Sounds silly, but it works.

The eyes have it

You already know that in any country, prolonged eye contact with a man is an invitation to flirt. In some developing countries or some societies, any eye contact at all may be considered carte blanche to approach you. Eye contact also may be considered disrespectful in some countries and may invite aggressive behavior from strangers. Almost as annoying is that eye contact ensures street buskers will pester you. Talk with local women to learn the rules.

WHAT TO DO IF TOUCHED OR GROPED

Say no

If you're being groped or touched inappropriately in a crowd, know how to say, "Leave me alone!" loudly in the local language. In Spanish, for instance, learn these useful phrases:

" De'jeme sola! (Leave me alone!)

" Vayase! (Go away!)

" Socorro! (Help!)

" Llama a la policia! Call the police!)

" Blast 'em if you must

Carry pepper spray in case of assault. Consider reporting this -- after all, you've just assaulted someone in the literal sense. Check in with the local embassy as soon as possible and let someone know what happened -- it's not always in your best interests to go to the police in some countries.

Remember to run

Always be ready to run like the wind (no high heels on deserted streets at night!).

WHAT TO DO IF YOU'RE BEING ASSAULTED

If you think you're going to be raped, a surprisingly effective tip from women travelers is to pretend you're going to vomit in the man's face - although a knee to the family jewels is sure to work, it may be grounds for arresting YOU for assault in some developing countries.

If you've been raped

It's not your fault. It's a crime, but it can be treated weirdly by some.

If you are raped, head for your hotel or a hospital to ask for help -- the police station may not be the best place to go, depending on your location. If you're raped by a member of your traveling group, grab a cab and head straight to the hospital.

Don't shower or douche before you get to the hospital. You may destroy evidence.

Women Traveler's Safety: Bottom Line

Look and act confident. Be alert. Use common sense. Always stride along like you know where you're going. Don't slink, glancing furtively around you.

Don't let all this scare you away from international travel - you'll doubtless be perfectly safe. Being young and female is great - enjoy it!

Chapter 10

NEW MARKET IN SOCIETIES

Aapravasi Ghat

The Immigration Depot (Hindi: Aapravasi Ghat) is a building complex located in Port Louis, on the Indian Ocean island of Mauritius, which was the first British colony to receive indentured, or contracted, labor workforce from India. From 1849 to 1923, half a million Indian indentured labourers passed through the Immigration Depot, to be eventually transported to plantations throughout the British Empire. The large-scale migration of the laborers left an indelible mark on the societies of many former British colonies, with Indians constituting a substantial proportion of their national populations. In Mauritius alone, 68 percent of the current total population has Indian forebearers. The Immigration Depot has thus become an important reference point in the history and cultural identity of Mauritius.

Unchecked infrastructural development in the mid-20th century however meant that only the partial remains of three stone buildings from the entire complex have survived. These are now protected as a national monument, under the Mauritian national heritage legislation. The Immigration Depot's role in social history has also been recognized by UNESCO when it was declared a World Heritage Site in 2006. The site is under the management of the

Aapravasi Ghat Trust Fund. Conservation efforts are underway to restore the fragile buildings back to their 1860s state.

Abu Mena

Abu Mena was a town, monastery complex and Christian pilgrimage center in Late Antique Egypt, about 45 km southwest of Alexandria. Its remains were designated a World Heritage Site in 1979. There are very few standing remains, but the foundations of most major buildings, such as the great basilica, are easily discernible. Recent agricultural efforts in the area have led to a significant rise in the water table, which has caused a number of the site's buildings to collapse or become unstable. The site was added to the list of threatened World Heritage Sites in 2001.

Aïr Mountains

he Aïr Mountains (also known as the Aïr Massif or Air of Niger; the name is Aya(r in Tuareg and Azbin /Abzin in eastern / western Hausa) is a triangular massif, located in northern Niger, within the Sahara desert. Part of the West Saharan montane xeric woodlands ecoregion, they rise to more than 6,000 ft (1 830 m) and extend over 84 000 km². Lying in the midst of desert north of the 17th parallel, the Aïr plateau, with an average altitude between 500 and 900 m, forms an island of Sahel climate which supports a wide variety of life, many pastoral and farming communities, and dramatic geological and archaeological sites. There are notable archaeological excavations in the region that illustrate the prehistoric past of this region. The endangered Painted Hunting Dog, Lycaon pictus once existed in Air of Niger region, but may now be extirpated due to human population pressures in this region.

Axum

Axum or Aksum is a city in northern Ethiopia which was the original capital of the eponymous kingdom of Axum. Axum was a naval and trading power that ruled the region from ca. 400 BC into the 10th century. The kingdom was also arbitrarily identified as Abyssinia, Ethiopia, and India in medieval writings.

Beni Hammad Fort

Beni Hammad Fort, also called Al Qal'a of Beni Hammad is a ruined fortified city in Algeria. It was the first capital of the Hammadid dynasty. It is located in the mountains northeast of M'Sila, near the town of Maadid (aka Maadhid), about 225 km southeast of Algiers. It was founded in 1007 and destroyed in 1152. In 1980, it was inscribed as a World Heritage Site by UNESCO, and described as "an authentic picture of a fortified Muslim city". The town include a 7 km-long line of walls and, among the buildings inside them, a mosque, the largest built in Algeria after that of Mansurah and similar to the Grand Mosque of Kairouan, with a tall minaret (20 m). The remains of the emir palace include three separate residences separated by gardens and pavilions. Excavations have brought to light numerous terracotta, jewels, coins and ceramics testifying the high level of civilization under the Hammadid dynasty.

Aldabra

Aldabra, the world's second largest coral atoll, is in the Aldabra Group of islands in the Indian Ocean that form part of the Seychelles. Uninhabited and extremely isolated Aldabra is virtually untouched by humans, has distinctive island fauna including the Aldabra Giant Tortoise, and is designated a World Heritage Site.

El Djem

El Djem is a town in Mahdia Governorate, Tunisia, population 18,302 (2004 census). It is home to some of the most impressive Roman remains in Africa.

The city was built, like almost all Roman settlements in Tunisia, on former Punic settlements. In a less arid climate than today's, Roman Thysdrus prospered especially in the 2nd century, when it became an important centre of olive oil manufacturing for export. It was the seat of a Christian bishop - which is still occupied by a titular Roman Catholic bishop today.

By the early 3rd century AD, when the amphitheatre was built, Thysdrus rivalled Hadrumetum (modern Sousse) as the second city of Roman North Africa, after Carthage. However, following the abortive revolt that began there in 238 AD, and Gordian I's suicide in his villa near Carthage, Roman troops loyal to the Emperor Maximinus Thrax destroyed the city. It never really recovered.

Ouadane

Ouadane is a town in northwestern Mauritania, lying on the Adrar Plateau, northeast of Chinguetti. It was founded in 1147 by the Berber tribe Idalwa el Hadji and soon became an important caravan and trading centre.

A Portuguese trading post was established in 1487, but the town declined from the sixteenth century. The old town, a World Heritage Site, though in ruins, is still substantially intact, while a small modern settlement lies outside its gate.

Thebes, Egypt

Thebes is the Greek name for a city in Ancient Egypt located about 800 km south of the Mediterranean, on the east bank of the river Nile. It was inhabited beginning in around 3200 BC. It was the eponymous capital of Waset, the fourth Upper Egyptian nome. Waset was the capital of Egypt during part of the 11th Dynasty (Middle Kingdom) and most of the 18th Dynasty (New Kingdom), when Hatshepsut built a Red Sea fleet to facilitate trade between Thebes Red Sea port of Elim, modern Quasir, and Elat at the head of the Gulf of Aqaba. Traders bought frankincense, myrrh, bitumen, natron, fine woven linen, juniper oil and copper amulets for the mortuary industry at Karnak with Nubian gold. With the 19th Dynasty the seat of government moved to the Delta. The archaeological remains of Thebes offer a striking testimony to Egyptian civilization at its height. The Greek poet Homer extolled the wealth of Thebes in the Iliad, Book 9 (c. 8th Century BC): "... in Egyptian Thebes the heaps of precious ingots gleam, the hundred-gated Thebes."

Carthage

Carthage refers to a series of cities on the Gulf of Tunis, from a Phoenician colony of the 1st millennium BCE to the current suburb outside Tunis, Tunisia. The first civilization that developed within the city's sphere of influence is referred to as Punic (a form of the word "Phoenician") or Carthaginian. The city of Carthage is located on the eastern side of Lake Tunis across from the centre of Tunis. According to Roman legend it was founded in 814 BCE by Phoenician colonists from Tyre under the leadership of Elissa (Queen Dido). It became a large and rich city and thus a major power in the Mediterranean. The resulting rivalry with Syracuse and Rome was accompanied by several wars with respective invasions of each other's homeland. Hannibal's invasion of Italy in the Second Punic War culminated in the Carthaginian victory at Cannae and led to a serious threat to the continuation of Roman rule over Italy; however, Carthage emerged from the conflict at its historical weakest after Hannibal's defeat at the Battle of Zama in 202 BCE. After the Third Punic War, the city was destroyed by the Romans in 146 BCE. However, the Romans refounded Carthage, which became one of the three most important cities of the Empire and the capital of the short-lived Vandal kingdom. It remained one of the most important Roman cities until the Muslim conquest when it was destroyed a second time in CE 698.

Cyrene, Libya

Cyrene was an ancient Greek colony in present-day Shahhat; Libya, the oldest and most important of the five Greek cities in the region. It gave eastern Libya the classical name Cyrenaica that it has retained to modern times. Cyrene lies in a lush valley in the Jebel Akhdar uplands. The city was named after a spring, Kyre, which the Greeks consecrated to Apollo. It was also the seat of the Cyrenaics, a famous school of philosophy in the 3rd century BC, founded by Aristippus, a disciple of Socrates.

Lepcis Magna

Leptis Magna, also known as Lectis Magna (or Lepcis Magna as it is sometimes spelled), also called Lpqy or Neapolis, was a prominent city of the Roman Empire. Its ruins are located in Al Khums, Libya, 130 km east of Tripoli, on the coast where the Wadi Lebda meets the sea. The site is one of the most spectacular and unspoiled Roman ruins in the Mediterranean. The city appears to have been founded by Phoenician colonists sometime around 1100 BC, although it did not achieve prominence until Carthage became a major power in the Mediterranean Sea in the 4th century BC. It nominally remained part of Carthage's dominions until the end of the Third Punic War in 146 BC and then became part of the Roman. Republic, although from about 200 BC onward, it was for all intents and purposes an independent city.

Sabratha

Sabratha, Sabratah or Siburata, in the Az Zawiyah District in the northwestern corner of modern Libya, was the westernmost of the "three cities" of Tripolis. From 2001 to 2007 it was the capital of the former Sabratha Wa Surman District. It lies on the Mediterranean coast about 65km (40 miles) west of Tripoli (ancient Oea). The extant archaeological site was inscribed as a UNESCO World Heritage Site in 1982.

Volubilis

Volubilis is an archaeological site in Morocco situated near Meknes between Fez and Rabat along the N13 road. The nearest town is Moulay Idriss. Volubilis features the best preserved ruins in this part of northern Africa. In 1997 the site was listed as a UNESCO World Heritage site.

Asante Traditional Buildings

Asante Traditional Buildings is a World Heritage Site in Ghana, which is a collection of 13 traditionally built buildings from the time of the Ashanti Empire in the area. The Asante Kingdom had its golden age in the 1700s, fell during the British occupation of the area from 1806 to 1901, and most Asante buildings of the period were destroyed during the area. Among other buildings, the royal mausoleum was destroyed by Baden-Powell in 1895. The buildings were described as "home of men and gods", and are the last remains of the history and culture of the Asante people. The houses are built of clay, straw and wood, and are vulnerable to natural fluctuations. There is therefore a need for the preservation of the buildings.

Banc d'Arguin National Park

The Banc d'Arguin National Park (French: Parc National du Banc d'Arguin) lies in Western Africa on the west coast of Mauritania between Nouakchott and Nouadhibou. The World Heritage Site is a major breeding site for migratory birds. A wide range of species include flamingos, broad-billed sandpipers, pelicans and terns. Much of the breeding is on sand banks including the islands of Tidra, Niroumi, Nair, Kijji and Arguim. The surrounding waters are some of the richest fishing waters in western Africa and serve as nesting grounds for the entire western region.

The Banc d'Arguin National Park is a Nature reserve that was established to protect both the natural resources and the valuable fisheries, which makes a significant contribution to the national economy (Hoffmann, 1988), as well as scientifically and aesthetically valuable geological sites, in the interests of and for the recreation of the general public. The park's vast expanses of mudflats provide a home for over two million migrant shorebirds from northern Europe, Siberia and Greenland. The region's mild climate and absence of human disturbance makes the park one of the most important sites in the world for these species. The nesting bird population is also noted for its great numbers and diversity. Between 25,000 and 40,000 pairs belonging to 15 species, making the largest colonies of water birds in West Africa (IUCN Technical Evaluation, 1989).

Bwindi Impenetrable National Park

Bwindi Impenetrable National Park is located in southwestern Uganda in East Africa. The park is part of the Bwindi Impenetrable Forest, and is situated along the Democratic Republic of Congo border next to the Virunga National Park and on the edge of the western Great Rift Valley. It comprises 331 square kilometres of jungle forests and contains both montane and lowland forest and is accessible only on foot. The Bwindi Impenetrable National Park is a UNESCO-designated World Heritage Site.

The forest is one of the richest ecosystems in Africa, and the diversity of species is a feature of the park. The park provides habitat for some 120 species of mammals, 346 species of birds, 202 species of butterflies, 163 species of trees, 100 species of ferns, 27 species of frogs, chameleons, geckos and many endangered species. In particular the area shares in the high levels of endemisms of the Albertine Rift.

The park is a sanctuary for colobus monkeys, chimpanzees and many birds (such as hornbills and turacos). It is perhaps most notable for the 340 Bwindi gorillas, half the world's population of the critically endangered Mountain Gorillas. There are four habituated Mountain Gorilla groups open to tourism: Mubare, Habinyanja, Rushegura near Buhoma; and the Nkuringo group at Nkuringo. Uganda Wildlife Authority leaflet, May 2008.

Cape Floristic Region

The Cape Floristic Region is a floristic region located near the southern tip of South Africa. It is the only floristic region of the Cape (South African) Floristic Kingdom, and includes only one floristic province, known as the Cape Floristic Province.

Chongoni Rock Art Area

Chongoni Rock Art Area is located in the Central Region of Malawi. This was inscribed as a UNESCO World Heritage Site in 2006.

Cidade Velha

Cidade Velha (Portuguese for "old city"), or simply Cidadi in Cape Verdean Creole, is a city located 15 km from Praia (Cape Verde's capital) on the island of Santiago. It is the oldest settlement in Cape Verde and used to serve as the capital of Cape Verde. Once called Ribeira Grande, its name was changed to Cidade Velha so to avoid confusion with another Ribeira Grande on another island. It is the seat of the Ribeira Grande de Santiago municipality. Located off of Africa's northwest coast, this city center was the first European colonial settlement in the tropics. Some of the meticulously planned original design of the site is still intact, from a royal fortress to two towering churches to a 16th-century town square. Today, Cidade Velha is an Atlantic shipping stop and center for Creole culture.

Bandiagara Escarpment

The Bandiagara Escarpment is an escarpment in the Dogon country of Mali. The sandstone cliff rises about 500 meters above the lower sandy flats to the south. It has a length of approximately 150 kilometers. The area of the escarpment is inhabited today by the Dogon people. Before the Dogon, the escarpment was inhabited by the Tellem and Toloy. Many structures remain from the Tellem. The Bandiagara Escarpment was listed in the UNESCO World Heritage List in 1989.The Cliffs of Bandiagara are a sandstone chain ranging from south to northeast over 200 km and extending to the Grandamia massif. The end of the massif is marked by the Hombori Tondo, Mali's highest peak at 1,115 meters. Because of its archaeological, ethnological and geological characteristics, the entire site is one of the most imposing in West Africa.

The cave-dwelling Tellem, an ethnic group later pushed out by the arrival of the Dogons, used to live in the slopes of the cliff. The Tellem legacy is evident in the caves they carved into the cliffs so that they could bury their dead high up, far from the frequent flash floods of the area. Dozens of villages are located along the cliff, such as Kani Bonzon. It was near to this village that the Dogons arrived in the 14th century, and from there they spread over the plateau, the escarpment and the plains of the Seno-Gondo.

There is an interesting theory explaining why the Dogon were relatively undisturbed by the French colonial powers. Supposedly there is a series of natural tunnels weaving through the Bandiagara Escarpment which only the Dogon know about, and they are able to use these caves to surprise and drive away any aggressors.

Today, local guides can take tourist groups on trips along the escarpment to visit the Dogon villages. A series of trails runs along the cliffs, and hostels in each village provide food and lodging. The host villages receive income from the hostels and the tourist tax.

Vast increases in tourism to the area are forecast to come, as a new highway is constructed, putting pressure on local, traditional cultures. In addition, The Independent reports that looting of ancient artifacts is widespread in the area and is poorly policed.

Comoé National Park

Comoé National Park is a national park in north eastern Côte d'Ivoire as well as a UNESCO World Heritage Site since its inscription in 1983. It is in the Ivoirian Zanzan Region between the towns of Kong to the west of both the park and the Comoé River, and Bouna to the east of the park, and just west of the Black Volta that forms the border, in that area, between Côte d'Ivoire and Burkina Faso. The park was initially added as a World Heritage Site due to the diversity of plant life present around the Comoé River, including pristine patches of tropical rain forest that are usually only found further south. As a well-eroded plain between two large rivers, the land in the area is home to soils and a moisture regime suitable to a richer biodiversity than surrounding areas. In 2003 it was added to the list of World Heritage Sites in Danger due to poaching, over-grazing of the park by cattle, and absence of management.

The floodplains around the River Comoé in Comoé National Park create seasonal grasslands that are the feeding grounds of a population of Hippopotamus amphibius. In addition, all three extant species of African crocodiles, Crocodylus niloticus, Mecistpos cataphractus, and Osteolaemus tetraspis, call parts of the park home, and migratory birds use the seasonal wetlands.

Dja Faunal Reserve

Dja Faunal Reserve, located in Cameroon, is a UNESCO World Heritage Site inscribed in 1987. Causes of inscription include diversity of species present in the park, the presence of five threatened species, and lack of disturbance within the park. The boundary that secludes the reserve is the Dja River, which almost completely surrounds it. There are more than 1,500 known plant species in the reserve, over 107 mammals more than 320 bird species in the park. The Dja Faunal Reserve covers 5,260 square kilometres (2,030 sq mi).

Djémila

Djemila (Tamazight: G(amila, Arabic: ??????, the Beautiful one, Latin: Cuicul or Curculum) is a mountain village in Algeria, near the northern coast east of Algiers, where some of the best preserved Berbero-Roman ruins in North Africa are found. It is situated in the region bordering the Constantinois and Petite Kabylie (Basse Kabylie).

Dejemila is a UNESCO World Heritage Site, and it was inscribed as such in 1982. It was recognized because of its unique adaptation of Roman architecture to a mountain environment. Buildings present in Djemila include a theatre, two fora, temples, basilicas, arches, streets, and houses. The exceptionally well preserved ruins organize themselves around the forum of the Harsh, a large paved square, the entry to which is marked by a majestic arch.

Djoudj National Bird Sanctuary

The Djoudj National Bird Sanctuary (French: Parc national des oiseaux du Djoudj) lies on the southeast bank of the River Senegal in Senegal, in northern Biffeche, north east of St-Louis. It provides a range of wetland habitats which prove very popular with migrating birds, many of which have just crossed the Sahara. Of almost 400 species of birds, the most visible are pelicans and flamingos. Less conspicuous are the Aquatic Warblers migrating here from Europe; for these, the park is the single most important wintering site yet discovered . A wide range of wildlife also inhabits the park, which is designated a World Heritage Site. The site was added to the list of World Heritage Sites in Danger in 2000 due to the introduction of the invasive giant salvinia plant, which threatens to choke out the park's native vegetation. However it was removed from the list in 2006

Dougga

Dougga or Thugga (Arabic: ????) is an ancient Roman city in northern Tunisia, included in a 65 hectare archaeological site.

UNESCO qualified Dougga as a World Heritage Site in 1997, believing that it represents "the best-preserved Roman small town in North Africa". The site, which lies in the middle of the countryside, has been protected from the encroachment of modern urbanisation, in contrast, for example, to Carthage, which has been pillaged and rebuilt on numerous occasions.

Dougga's size, its well-preserved monuments and its rich Punic, Numidian, ancient Roman and Byzantine history make it exceptional. Amongst the most famous monuments at the site are a Punic-Libyan mausoleum, the capitol, the theatre, and the temples of Saturn and of Juno Caelestis.

Lopé National Park

Lopé National Park is a national park in central Gabon. Although the terrain is mostly rain forest, in the north the park contains the last remnants of grass savannas created in Central Africa during the last Ice Age, 15,000 years ago. It was the first protected area in Gabon when the Lopé-Okanda Wildlife Reserve was created in 1946. In 2007, the Lopé-Okanda landscape was added to the World Heritage List by UNESCO.

The park contains a small research station, named as Mikongo and run by the Zoological Society London, based in the village known as Mikongo, from which it gets its name. There exists infrastructure to cater for tourists at the base, including several chalets and a large open air dining room, from which the rainforest is a mere five meters away.

Fasil Ghebbi

Fasil Ghebbi is a fortress-enclosure located in Gondar, Ethiopia. It served as the home of Ethiopia's emperors in the 17th and 18th centuries. Its unique architecture shows diverse influences including Nubian, Arab, and Baroque styles. The site was inscribed as a UNESCO World Heritage Site in 1979. This complex of buildings includes Fasilides castle, Iyasu's Palace, Dawit's Hall, a banqueting hall, stables, Mentewab's Castle, a chancellery, library and three churches.

Forts and Castles, Volta, Greater Accra, Central and Western Regions

The site features the remains of fortified trading posts, built along the coast between Keta and Bayin between 1482 and 1786.

Cradle of Humankind

The Cradle of Humankind is a World Heritage Site first named by UNESCO in 1999, about 50 kilometres northwest of Johannesburg, South Africa in the Gauteng province. This site currently occupies 47,000 hectares (180 sq mi); it contains a complex of limestone caves, including the Sterkfontein Caves, where the 2.3-million year-old fossil Australopithecus africanus (nicknamed "Mrs. Ples") was found in 1947 by Dr. Robert Broom and John T. Robinson. The find helped corroborate the 1924 discovery of the juvenile Australopithecus africanus skull, "Taung Child", by Raymond Dart, at Taung in the North West Province of South Africa, where excavations still continue.

The name Cradle of Humankind reflects the fact that the site has produced a large number, as well as some of the oldest, hominid fossils ever found, some dating back as far as 3.5 million years ago. Sterkfontein alone has produced more than a third of early hominid fossils ever found.

Garajonay National Park

Garajonay National Park (Spanish: Parque nacional de Garajonay) is located in the center and north of the island of La Gomera, one of the Canary Islands (Spain). It was declared a national park in 1981 and a World Heritage Site by UNESCO in 1986. It occupies 40 km2 (15 sq mi) and it extends into each of the municipalities on the island.

The park is named after the rock formation of Garajonay, the highest point on the island at 1,484 m (4,869 feet). It also includes a small plateau whose altitude is 790-1,400 m (2,600-4,600 feet) above sea level.

The park provides the best example of laurisilva, a humid subtropical forest that in the Tertiary covered almost all of Europe. It is also found on the Azores and the Madeira Islands. Laurus azorica, known as Azores Laurel, or by the Portuguese names Louro, Loureiro, Louro-da-terra, and Louro-de-cheiro, can be found in the park, as well as Laurus canariensis, known as Canary Laurel. Although named as a single type of forest, the National Park englobes several varieties of forests. Most humid and protected valleys oriented to the North have the richest and complex forests. It is called valley laurisilva, a true subtropical rainforest where the largest laurel trees can be found. As we reach higher mounts, with less protection from wind and sun, the forest loses some of its more delicate species. It is called the slope laurisilva (laurisilva de ladera). At the south the forest is mainly a mix of beech and heather, species adapted to the less humid atmosphere.

Other attractive of the National Park is the massive rocks that are found along the island. These are former volcanos whose shape has been sharpened by erosion. Some, like the "Fortaleza" (fortress in spanish) were considered sacred by the aborigins, as well as ideal refugees when attached. The park is crossed with a large network of footpaths, being trekking one of the main touristic activities in the island.

Many of the species are endemic to the islands, and harbor a rich biota of understory plants, invertebrates, and birds and bats, including a number of endemic species.

Two species of reptile, Gallotia gomerana (Gomeran lizard) and Chalcides viridanus (Gomeran skink), can be found. Amphibians include the stripeless tree frog, Hyla meridionalis.

The park is renowned as one of the best places to observe the two Canarian endemic pigeons, Laurel Pigeon (Columba junoniae) and Bolle's Pigeon (Columba bollii).

Garamba National Park

Garamba National Park, located in the Democratic Republic of the Congo in Africa, was established in 1938. One of Africa's oldest National parks, it was designated a UNESCO World Heritage Site in 1980. Garamba is (or at least was) the home to the world's last known wild population of Northern White Rhinoceros. Due to poaching of the rhinos within the park, it was added to the list of World Heritage Sites in danger in 1996. The park is also well known for its African elephant domestication programme started in the 1960s, which managed to train tourist-rideable animals from the naturally wild beasts.

Kairouan

Kairouan is the capital of the Kairouan Governorate in Tunisia. Referred to as the Islamic Cultural Capital, it is considered the fourth most holy city in Islam, and is a UNESCO World Heritage site. The city was founded by the Arabs around 670 in the period of Caliph Mu'awiya, becoming an important center for Islamic and Quranic learning, and thus attracting a large number of Muslims from various parts of the world, next only to Mecca and Medina. The holy Mosque of Uqba is situated in the city. In 2003 the city had about 150,000 inhabitants.

Aït Benhaddou

Aït Benhaddou is a 'fortified city', or ksar, along the former caravan route between the Sahara and Marrakech in present-day Morocco. It is situated in Souss-Massa-Draâ on a hill along the Ounila River and has some beautiful examples of kasbahs, which unfortunately sustain damage during each rainstorm. Most of the town's inhabitants now live in a more modern village at the other side of the river; however, ten families still live within the ksar.

Kingdom of Mapungubwe

The Kingdom of Mapungubwe (1075-1220) was a pre-colonial Southern African state located at the confluence of the Shashe and Limpopo rivers south of Great Zimbabwe. It marked the center of a pre-Shona kingdom which covered parts of modern-day Botswana and Zimbabwe and South Africa. The kingdom was the first stage in a development that would culminate in the creation of the Kingdom of Zimbabwe in the 13th century.

Memphis, Egypt

Memphis was the ancient capital of Aneb-Hetch, the first nome of Lower Egypt. Its ruins are located near the town of Helwan, south of Cairo. According to legend related by Manetho, the city was founded by the pharaoh Menes around 3000 BCE. Capital of

Egypt during the Old Kingdom, it remained an important city throughout ancient Mediterranean history. It occupied a strategic position at the mouth of the Nile delta, and was home to feverish activity. Its principal port, Peru-nefer, harboured a high density of workshops, factories, and warehouses that distributed food and merchandise throughout the ancient kingdom. During its golden age, Memphis thrived as a regional centre for commerce, trade, and religion.

Memphis was believed to be under the protection of the god Ptah, the patron of craftsmen. Its great temple, Hout-ka-Ptah (meaning "Castle of the ka of Ptah"), was one of the most prominent structures in the city. The name of this temple, rendered in Greek as by the historian Manetho, is believed to be the etymological origin of the modern English name Egypt. The history of Memphis is closely linked to that of the country itself. Its eventual downfall is believed to be due to the loss of its economical significance in late antiquity, following the rise of coastal Alexandria. Its religious significance also diminished after the abandonment of the ancient religion following the Edict of Thessalonica. The ruins of the former capital today offer fragmented evidence of its magnificent past. They have been preserved, along with the pyramid complex at Giza, as a World Heritage Site since 1979. The site is open to the public as an open-air museum.

Giza Necropolis

The Giza Necropolis stands on the Giza Plateau, on the outskirts of Cairo, Egypt. This complex of ancient monuments includes the three pyramid complexes known as the Great Pyramids, the massive sculpture known as the Great Sphinx, other smaller tombs, a workers' village and an industrial complex. It is located some 9 Km (5 mi) inland into the desert from the old town of Giza on the Nile, some 25 Km (15 mi) southwest of Cairo city centre. One of the iconic monuments, the Great Pyramid of Giza, is the only remaining monument of the Seven Wonders of the Ancient World.

Timbuktu

Timbuktu is a city in Tombouctou Region, in the West African nation of Mali. It was made prosperous by the tenth mansa of the

Mali Empire, Mansa Musa. It is home to Sankore University and other madrasas, and was an intellectual and spiritual capital and centre for the propagation of Islam throughout Africa in the 15th and 16th centuries. Its three great mosques, Djingareyber, Sankore and Sidi Yahya, recall Timbuktu's golden age. Although continuously restored, these monuments are today under threat from desertification.

Populated by Songhay, Tuareg, Fulani, and Mandé people, Timbuktu is about 15 km north of the Niger River. It is also at the intersection of an east–west and a north–south Trans-Saharan trade route across the Sahara to Araouane. It was important historically (and still is today) as an entrepot for rock-salt originally from Taghaza, now from Taoudenni.

Its geographical setting made it a natural meeting point for nearby west African populations and nomadic Berber and Arab peoples from the north. Its long history as a trading outpost that linked west Africa with Berber, Arab, and Jewish traders throughout north Africa, and thereby indirectly with traders from Europe, has given it a fabled status, and in the West it was for long a metaphor for exotic, distant lands: "from here to Timbuktu."

Timbuktu's long-lasting contribution to Islamic and world civilization is scholarship. Timbuktu is assumed to have had one of the first universities in the world. Local scholars and collectors still boast an impressive collection of ancient Greek texts from that era. By the 14th century, important books were written and copied in Timbuktu, establishing the city as the centre of a significant written tradition in Africa.

Cueva de las Manos

Cueva de las Manos (Spanish for Cave of the Hands) is a cave or a series of caves located in the province of Santa Cruz, Argentina, 163 km (101 mi) south of the town of Perito Moreno. It is famous (and gets its name) for the paintings of hands, made by the indigenous inhabitants (possibly forefathers of the Tehuelches) some 9,000 years ago. The composition of the inks is mineral, so the age of the paintings was calculated from the remains of bone-made pipes used for spraying the paint on the wall blocked by the hand.

The cave lies in the valley of the Pinturas River, in an isolated spot in the Patagonian landscape. It is most easily reached by a gravel road (RP 41), which leaves Ruta 40 3 km north of Bajo Caracoles and runs 46 km northeast to the south side of the Pinturas Canyon. The north side of the canyon can also be reached by rough, but shorter, roads from Ruta 40. A 3 km path connects the two sides of the canyon, but there is no road link.

The main cave measures 24 m (79 ft) in depth, with an entrance 15 m (49 ft) wide, and it is initially 10 m (33 ft) high. The ground inside the cave has an upward slope; inside the cave the height is reduced to no more than 2 m (7 ft).

The images of hands are often negative (stencilled). Besides these there are also depictions of human beings, guanacos, rheas, felines and other animals, as well as geometric shapes, zigzag patterns, representations of the sun, and hunting scenes. Similar paintings, though in smaller numbers, can be found in nearby caves. There are also red dots on the ceilings, probably made by submerging their hunting bolas in ink, and then throwing them up. The colours of the paintings vary from red (made from hematite) to white, black or yellow. The negative hand impressions are calculated to be dated around 550 BC, the positive impressions from 180 BC, and the hunting drawings to be older than 10,000 years

Most of the hands are left hands, which suggests that painters held the spraying pipe with their dexterous hand. The size of the hands resembles that of a 13-year-old boy, but considering they were probably smaller in size, it is speculated that they could be a few years older, and marked their advancement into manhood by stamping their hands on the walls of this sacred cave.

Cueva de las Manos has been listed as a World Heritage Site since 1999.

Los Glaciares National Park

Parque Nacional Los Glaciares (Spanish: The Glaciers) is a national park in the Santa Cruz Province, in Argentine Patagonia. It comprises an area of 4459 km². In 1981 it was declared a World Heritage Site by UNESCO.

The national park, created in 1937, is the second largest in Argentina. Its name refers to the giant ice cap in the Andes range that feeds 47 large glaciers, of which only 13 flow towards the Atlantic Ocean. The ice cap is the largest outside of Antarctica and Greenland. In other parts of the world, glaciers start at a height of at least 2,500 meters above mean sea level, but due to the size of the ice cap, these glaciers begin at only 1,500m, sliding down to 200m AMSL, eroding the surface of the mountains that support them.

Belize Barrier Reef

The Belize Barrier Reef is a series of coral reefs straddling the coast of Belize, roughly 300 meters (1,000 ft) offshore in the north and 40 kilometers (25 mi) in the south within the country limits. The Belize Barrier Reef is a 300 kilometers (186 mi) long section of the 900 kilometers (560 mi) long Mesoamerican Barrier Reef System, which is continuous from Cancún on the northeast tip of the Yucatán Peninsula through the Riviera Maya up to Honduras, making it the second largest coral reef system in the world after the Great Barrier Reef in Australia, popular for scuba diving and snorkeling. It is Belize's top tourist destination, attracting almost half of its 260,000 visitors, and vital to its fishing industry.

Charles Darwin described it as "the most remarkable reef in the West Indies" in 1842.

El Fuerte de Samaipata

El Fuerte de Samaipata (English: Fort Samaipata), also known simply as 'El Fuerte', is an archaeological site and UNESCO World Heritage Site located in the Santa Cruz Department, Florida Province, Bolivia..It is situated in the eastern foothills of the Bolivian Andes, and is a popular tourist destination for Bolivians and foreigners alike. It is served by the nearby town of Samaipata.

It is not actually a military fortification but it is generally considered a pre-Columbian religious site, built by the Chanes, a pre-Inca culture of Arawak origin. There are also ruins of an Inca city built near the temple; the city was built during the Inca expansion to the southeast. Both Incas and Chanes suffered several raids from

Guarani warriors that invaded the region from time to time. Eventually, the Guarani warriors conquered the plains and valleys of Santa Cruz and destroyed Samaipata. The Guaranis dominated the region well into the Spanish colonial period.

The Spaniards also built a settlement near the temple and there are remains of buildings of typical Arab Andalusian architecture. The Spaniards abandoned the settlement and moved to the nearby valley were the town of Samaipata is currently located.

The archeological site at El Fuerte is unique and it encompasses buildings of three different cultures: Chanes, Incas and Spaniards.

Noel Kempff Mercado National Park

Noel Kempff Mercado National Park is a national park in the north-eastern portion of the Santa Cruz Department, Province of José Miguel de Velasco, Bolivia, on the border with Brazil. The date of its foundation was on June 28, 1979. Its original name was "Parque Nacional Huanchaca", but was then changed to "Parque Nacional Noel Kempff Mercado" in honor of the late pioneering biologist and Bolivian conservationist Prof. Noel Kempff Mercado, for his research and discoveries in the Park - and also in memory of his tragic death in the area; In 1988 Mercado was murdered here by drug traffickers after stumbling across a secret cocaine laboratory high on the Huanchaca plateau.

Serra do Mar

Serra do Mar (Portuguese: for Mountain Range of the Sea) is a 1,500 km long system of mountain ranges and escarpments in Southeastern Brazil, which runs in parallel to the Atlantic Ocean coast, from the state of São Paulo to Paraná. The main escarpment forms the boundary between the sea-level littoral and the inland plateau (planalto), which has a mean altitude of 500 to 1300 m. The mountain ranges are discontinuous in several places and receive individual names, such as Serra de Bocaina, Serra de Paranapiacaba, Serra Negra, Serra do Indaiá, etc. It also extends to some large islands near the coastline, such as Ilhabela and Ilha Anchieta. The highest point of Serra do Mar is the Pico Paraná, located in the municipalities of Antonina and Campina Grande do Sul Rio de Janeiro in Nova Friburgo Pico da Caledônia with altitude of 2.255 meters or 7398.293 feet.

Geologically, the Serra do Mar belongs to the massive crystalline rock platform that forms Eastern South America and tectonically is very stable. Most of the elevations of Serra do Mar were formed about 60 million years ago.

At the time of discovery of Brazil (1500), Serra do Mar supported a rich and highly diversified ecosystem, composed mainly by a lush tropical rain forest, called Mata Atlântica (Atlantic Rainforest). Due to urbanization and deforestation, however, most of the forest cover was destroyed and it remains almost exclusively in the steep escarpments facing the sea. A chain of national and state parks, ecological stations and biological reservations now protect the Mata Atlântica and its biological heritage, but acid rain, pollution, poachers, clandestine loggers, forest fires and encroachment by urban areas and farms are still promoting active destruction, particularly around cities. The largest metropolis of São Paulo and Curitiba are near the Serra do Mar.

Reforestation and recuperation of biological diversity are notoriously difficult to bring about in destroyed rain forest habitats.

Atlantic Forest

The Atlantic Forest (Portuguese: 'Mata Atlântica') is a region of tropical and subtropical moist forest, tropical dry forest, tropical savannas, and mangrove forests which extends along the Atlantic coast of Brazil from Rio Grande do Norte state in the north to Rio Grande do Sul state in the south, and inland as far as Paraguay and the Misiones Province of Argentina.

The Atlantic Forest region includes forests of several variations.

- The coastal restingas are low forests which grow on stabilized coastal dunes.
- The coastal forests, also known as Atlantic moist forests, are evergreen tropical forests with structures.
- Inland are the interior forests, also known as the Atlantic semi-deciduous forests, where many trees drop their leaves during the dry season.

- Further inland are the Atlantic dry forests, which form a transition between the arid Caatinga to the northeast and the Cerrado savannas to the east.
- Montane moist forests occur in the Serra do Mar and across the mountains and plateaus of southern Brazil, and are home to Araucaria and evergreen trees of the laurel (Lauraceae) and myrtle (Myrtaceae) families.
- Shrubby montane savannas occur at the highest elevations.

The Atlantic Forest is unusual in that it extends as a true tropical rainforest to latitudes as high as 24°S. This is because the trade winds produce precipitation throughout the southern winter. In fact, the northern Zona da Mata of northeastern Brazil receives much more rainfall between May and August than during the southern summer.

The Atlantic Forest is now designated a World Biosphere Reserve, which contains a large number of highly endangered species including the well known marmosets and lion tamarins. It has been extensively cleared since colonial times, mainly for the farming of sugar cane and for urban settlements. The remnant is estimated to be less than 10% of the original and that is often broken into hilltop islands.

The Amazon Institute is active in reforestation efforts in the northeastern state of Pernambuco, Brazil. During 2007, Joao Milanez and Joanne Stanulonis have planted 5,500 new trees in the mountains commencing with Gravata, adding to the precious little, ancient forest left.

During glacial periods, however, the Atlantic Forest is known to have shrunk to extremely small refugia in highly sheltered gullies, with most of the land area more recently occupied by the characteristic Atlantic Forest being occupied by dry forest or even semi-desert. Some maps even suggest the forest actually survived in moist pockets well away from the coastline, where its endemic rainforest species mixed with much cooler-climate species. Unlike refugia for equatorial rainforests, the refuges for the Atlantic Forest have never been the product of detailed identification.

Area de Conservación Guanacaste World Heritage Site

The Area de Conservación Guanacaste, is a World Heritage Site in the northwestern part of Costa Rica, which comprises Santa Rosa, Guanacaste, Rincón de la Vieja National Parks and the Junquillal Bay Wildlife Refuge. It formally became part of National System of Conservation Areas (SINAC) in 1994, and then a World Heritage site in 1999. The area of the parks combined totals 1470 square kilometers as of 2004.

Hanging Gardens of Babylon

The Hanging Gardens of Babylon are considered to be one of the original Seven Wonders of the Ancient World. They were built in the ancient city-state of Babylon, near present-day Al Hillah, Babil, in Iraq. They are sometimes called the Hanging Gardens of Semiramis (in reference to the legendary Queen Semiramis).

The gardens were supposedly built by the Babylonian king Nebuchadnezzar II around 600 BC. He is reported to have constructed the gardens to please his homesick wife, Amytis of Media, who longed for the trees and fragrant plants of her homeland Persia. The gardens were destroyed by several earthquakes after the second century BC.

The lush Hanging Gardens are extensively documented by Greek historians such as Strabo and Diodorus Siculus. Through the ages, the location may have been confused with gardens that existed at Nimrud, since tablets from there clearly show gardens. Writings on these tablets describe the possible use of something similar to an Archimedes screw as a process of raising the water to the required height. Nebuchadnezzar II also used massive slabs of stone, which was unheard of in Babylon, to prevent the water from eroding the ground.

Statue of Zeus at Olympia

The Statue of Zeus at Olympia was made by the Greek sculptor Phidias, circa 432 BC on the site where it was erected in the Temple of Zeus, Olympia, Greece. It was one of the Seven Wonders of the Ancient World.

Temple of Artemis

The Temple of Artemis, also known less precisely as Temple of Diana, was a Greek temple dedicated to a goddess Greeks identified as Artemis that was completed, in its most famous phase, around 550 BC at Ephesus (in present-day Turkey). Though the monument was one of the Seven Wonders of the Ancient World, only foundations and sculptural fragments of the temple remain. There were previous temples on its site, where evidence of a sanctuary dates as early as the Bronze Age. The whole temple was made of marble except for the roof.

The temple antedated the Ionic immigration by many years. Callimachus, in his Hymn to Artemis, attributed the origin of the temenos at Ephesus to the Amazons, whose worship he imagines already centered upon an image. In the seventh century the old temple was destroyed by a flood. The construction of the "new" temple, which was to become known as one of the wonders of the ancient world, began around 550 BC. It was a 120-year project, initially designed and built by the Cretan architect Chersiphron and his son Metagenes, at the expense of Croesus of Lydia.

It was described by Antipater of Sidon, who compiled the list of the Seven Wonders:

I have set eyes on the wall of lofty Babylon on which is a road for chariots, and the statue of Zeus by the Alpheus, and the hanging gardens, and the colossus of the Sun, and the huge labour of the high pyramids, and the vast tomb of Mausolus; but when I saw the house of Artemis that mounted to the clouds, those other marvels lost their brilliancy, and I said, "Lo, apart from Olympus, the Sun never looked on aught so grand".

Mausoleum of Halicarnassus

The Mausoleum at Halicarnassus or Tomb of Mausolus was a tomb built between 353 and 350 BC at Halicarnassus (present Bodrum, Turkey) for Mausolus, a satrap in the Persian Empire, and Artemisia II of Caria, his wife and sister. The structure was designed by the Greek architects Satyros and Pythis. It stood approximately 45 m (148 ft) in height, and each of the four sides was adorned with sculptural reliefs created by each one of four Greek sculptors — Leochares, Bryaxis, Scopas of Paros and Timotheus. The finished structure was considered to be such an aesthetic triumph that Antipater of Sidon identified it as one of his Seven Wonders of the Ancient World. The word mausoleum has since come to be used generically for any grand tomb.

Colossus of Rhodes

The Colossus of Rhodes was a statue of the Greek god Helios, erected in the city of Rhodes on the Greek island of Rhodes by Chares of Lindos between 292 and 280 BC. It is considered one of the Seven Wonders of the Ancient World. Before its destruction, the Colossus of Rhodes stood over 30 meters (107 ft) high, making it one of the tallest statues of the ancient world.

Lighthouse of Alexandria

The Lighthouse of Alexandria, also known as the Pharos of Alexandria, was a tower built between 280 and 247 BC on the island of Pharos at Alexandria, Egypt to guide sailors into the harbour at night. With a height variously estimated at between 393 and 450 ft (120 and 140 m), it was for many centuries among the tallest man-made structures, and was one of the Seven Wonders of the Ancient World.

Stonehenge

Stonehenge is a prehistoric monument located in the English county of Wiltshire, about 3.2 kilometres (2.0 mi) west of Amesbury and 13 kilometres (8.1 mi) north of Salisbury. One of the most famous sites in the world, Stonehenge is composed of earthworks surrounding a circular setting of large standing stones. It is at the centre of the most dense complex of Neolithic and Bronze Age monuments in England, including several hundred burial mounds.

Archaeologists had believed that the iconic stone monument was erected around 2500 BC, as described in the chronology below. One recent theory, however, has suggested that the first stones were not erected until 2400-2200 BC, whilst another suggests that bluestones may have been erected at the site as early as 3000 BC (see phase 1 below). The surrounding circular earth bank and ditch, which constitute the earliest phase of the monument, have been dated to about 3100 BC. The site and its surroundings were added to the UNESCO's list of World Heritage Sites in 1986 in a co-listing with Avebury Henge monument. It is a national legally protected Scheduled Ancient Monument. Stonehenge is owned by the Crown and managed by English Heritage, while the surrounding land is owned by the National Trust.

Archaeological evidence found by the Stonehenge Riverside Project in 2008 indicates that Stonehenge served as a burial ground from its earliest beginnings. The dating of cremated remains found on the site indicate burials from as early as 3000 BC, when the initial ditch and bank were first dug. Burials continued at Stonehenge for at least another 500 years.

COLOSSEUM

The Colosseum or, The Coliseum, originally the Flavian Amphitheatre (Latin: Amphitheatrum Flavium, Italian Anfiteatro Flavio or Colosseo), is an elliptical amphitheatre in the center of the city of Rome, Italy, the largest ever built in the Roman Empire. It is considered one of the greatest works of Roman architecture and Roman engineering.

Occupying a site just east of the Roman Forum, its construction started between 70 and 72 AD under the emperor Vespasian and was completed in 80 AD under Titus, with further modifications being made during Domitian's reign (81–96). The name "Amphitheatrum Flavium" derives from both Vespasian's and Titus's family name (Flavius, from the gens Flavia).

Capable of seating 50,000 spectators, the Colosseum was used for gladiatorial contests and public spectacles such as mock sea battles, animal hunts, executions, re-enactments of famous battles, and dramas based on Classical mythology. The building ceased to be used for entertainment in the early medieval era. It was later reused for such purposes as housing, workshops, quarters for a religious order, a fortress, a quarry, and a Christian shrine.

Although in the 21st century it stays partially ruined because of damage caused by devastating earthquakes and stone-robbers, the Colosseum is an iconic symbol of Imperial Rome. It is one of Rome's most popular tourist attractions and still has close connections with the Roman Catholic Church, as each Good Friday the Pope leads a torchlit "Way of the Cross" procession that starts in the area around the Colosseum.

The Colosseum is also depicted on the Italian version of the five-cent euro coin.

Catacombs of Kom el Shoqafa

The Catacombs of Kom el Shoqafa (meaning 'Mound of shards' or 'Potsherds') is a historical archaeological site located in Alexandria, Egypt and is considered one of the Seven Wonders of the Middle Ages.

The necropolis consists of a series of Alexandrian tombs, statues and archaeological objects of the Pharaonic funeral cult with Hellenistic and early Imperial Roman influences. Due to the time period, many of the features of the Catacombs of Kom el Shoqafa merge Roman, Greek and Egyptian cultural points; some statues are Egyptian in style, yet bear Roman clothes and hair style whilst other features share a similar style. A circular staircase, which was often used to transport deceased bodies down the middle of it, leads down into the tombs that were tunneled into the bedrock during the age of the Antonine emperors (2nd century AD). The facility was then used as a burial chamber from the 2nd century to the 4th century, before being rediscovered in 1900 when a donkey accidentally fell into the access shaft. To date, three sarcophagi have been found, along with other human and animal remains which were added later. It is believed that the catacombs were only intended for a single family, but it is unclear why the site was expanded in order to house numerous other individuals. The Catacombs of Kom el Shoqafa is, according to some lists, also one of the seven medieval wonders of the world. One of the more gruesome features of the catacombs is the so called Hall of Caracalla. According to tradition, this is a mass burial chamber for the humans and animals massacred by order of the Emperor Caracalla.

Great Wall of China

The Great Wall of China is a series of stone and earthen fortifications in northern China, built originally to protect the northern borders of the Chinese Empire against intrusions by various nomadic groups. Several walls have been built since the 5th century BC that are referred to collectively as the Great Wall, which has been rebuilt and maintained from the 5th century BC through the 16th century. One of the most famous is the wall built between 220–206 BC by the first Emperor of China, Qin Shi Huang. Little of that wall remains; the majority of the existing wall was built during the Ming Dynasty.

The Great Wall stretches from Shanhaiguan in the east, to Lop Nur in the west, along an arc that roughly delineates the southern edge of Inner Mongolia. The most comprehensive archaeological survey, using advanced technologies, has recently concluded that the entire Great Wall, with all of its branches, stretches for 8,851.8 km (5,500.3 mi). This is made up of 6,259.6 km (3,889.5 mi) sections of actual wall, 359.7 km (223.5 mi) of trenches and 2,232.5 km (1,387.2 mi) of natural defensive barriers such as hills and rivers.

Porcelain Tower of Nanjing

The Porcelain Tower is a historical site located on the south bank of the Yangtze in Nanjing, China. It was a pagoda constructed in the 15th century during the Ming Dynasty, but was mostly destroyed in the 19th century during the course of the Taiping Rebellion. The tower is now under reconstruction.

The tower was octagonal with a base of about 97 feet (30 m) in diameter. When it was built, the tower was one of the largest buildings in China, rising up to a height of 260 feet (79 m) with nine stories and a staircase in the middle of the pagoda, which spiraled upwards for 184 steps. The top of the roof was marked by a golden pineapple. There were originally plans to add more stories, according to an American missionary who in 1852 visited Nanjing. There are only a few Chinese pagodas that surpass its height, such as the still existent 275-foot-tall (84 m) 11th-century Liaodi Pagoda in Hebei or the no longer existent 330-foot-tall (100 m) 7th-century wooden pagoda of Chang'an.

The tower was built with white porcelain bricks that were said to reflect the sun's rays during the day, and at night as many as 140 lamps were hung from the building to illuminate the tower. Glazes and stoneware were worked into the porcelain and created a mixture of green, yellow, brown and white designs on the sides of the tower, including animals, flowers and landscapes. The tower was also decorated with numerous Buddhist images.

HAGIA SOPHIA

Hagia Sophia is a former Orthodox patriarchal basilica, later a mosque and now a museum in Istanbul, Turkey. From the date of its dedication in 360 until 1453, it served as the cathedral of Constantinople, except between 1204 and 1261, when it was the cathedral of the Latin Empire. The building was a mosque from 29 May 1453 until 1934, when it was secularized. It was opened as a museum on 1 February 1935.

The Church was dedicated to the Logos, the second Person of the Holy Trinity. This is confirmed by its Dedication's Feast, which took place on December 25th, the anniversary of the Incarnation of the Logos in Christ.

Famous in particular for its massive dome, it is considered the epitome of Byzantine architecture and is said to have "changed the history of architecture." It was the largest cathedral in the world for nearly a thousand years, until Seville Cathedral was completed in 1520. The current building was originally constructed as a church between 532 and 537 on the orders of the Byzantine Emperor Justinian and was the third Church of the Holy Wisdom to occupy the site, the previous two having both been destroyed by rioters. It was designed by Isidore of Miletus, a physicist, and Anthemius of Tralles, a mathematician.

The church contained a large collection of holy relics and featured, among other things, a 49 foot (15 m) silver iconostasis. It was the seat of the Patriarch of Constantinople and the religious focal point of the Eastern Orthodox Church for nearly one thousand years. It is the church in which Cardinal Humbert in 1054 excommunicated Michael I Cerularius - which is commonly considered the start of the Great Schism.

In 1453, Constantinople was conquered by the Ottoman Turks and Sultan Mehmed II ordered the building to be converted into a mosque. The bells, altar, iconostasis, and sacrificial vessels were removed and many of the mosaics were eventually plastered over. The Islamic features — such as the mihrab, the minbar, and the four minarets outside — were added over the course of its history under the Ottomans. It remained as a mosque until 1935, when it was converted into a museum by the Republic of Turkey.

For almost 500 years the principal mosque of Istanbul, Hagia Sophia served as a model for many other Ottoman mosques, such as the Sultan Ahmed Mosque (Blue Mosque of Istanbul), the S,ehzade Mosque, the Süleymaniye Mosque, the Rüstem Pasha Mosque and the K?l?ç Ali Pas,a Mosque.

Although it is sometimes referred to as Sancta Sophia, as though it were named after a saint named Sophia, Church of the Holy Wisdom of God, the church being dedicated to Jesus Christ, in Eastern Orthodox theology, the Holy Wisdom of God.

Leaning Tower of Pisa

The Leaning Tower of Pisa (Italian: Torre pendente di Pisa) or simply the Tower of Pisa (La Torre di Pisa) is the campanile, or freestanding bell tower, of the cathedral of the Italian city of Pisa. It is situated behind the Cathedral and is the third oldest structure in Pisa's Cathedral Square (Piazza del Duomo) after the Cathedral and the Baptistry.

Although intended to stand vertically, the tower began leaning to the southeast soon after the onset of construction in 1173 due to a poorly laid foundation and loose substrate that has allowed the foundation to shift direction. The tower currently leans to the southwest.

The height of the tower is 55.86 m (183.27 ft) from the ground on the lowest side and 56.70 m (186.02 ft) on the highest side. The width of the walls at the base is 4.09 m (13.42 ft) and at the top

2.48 m (8.14 ft). Its weight is estimated at 14,500 metric tons (16,000 short tons). The tower has 296 or 294 steps; the seventh floor has two fewer steps on the north-facing staircase. Prior to restoration work performed between 1990 and 2001, the tower leaned at an angle of 5.5 degrees, but the tower now leans at about 3.99 degrees. This means that the top of the tower is 3.9 metres (12 ft 10 in) from where it would stand if the tower were perfectly vertical.

Cairo Citadel

The Saladin Citadel of Cairo is a fortification in Cairo, Egypt. The location, part of the Muqattam hill near the center of Cairo, was once famous for its fresh breeze and grand views of the city, and was fortified by the Ayyubid ruler Salah al-Din (Saladin) between 1176 and 1183 AD, to protect it from the Crusaders.

Only a few years after defeating the Fatimid Caliphate, Saladin set out to build a wall that would surround both Cairo and Fustat. Saladin is recorded as saying, "With a wall I will make the two [cities of Cairo and Fustat] into a unique whole, so that one army may defend them both; and I believe it good to encircle them with a single wall from the bank of the Nile to the bank of the Nile." The Citadel would be the centerpiece of the wall. Built on a promontory beneath the Muqattam Hills, a setting that made it difficult to attack, the efficacy of the Citadel's location is further demonstrated by the fact that it remained the heart of Egyptian government until the nineteenth century. . The citadel stopped being the seat of government when Egypt's ruler, Khedive Ismail, moved to his newly built Abdin Palace in the Ismailiya neighborhood in the 1860s.

While the Citadel was completed in 1183-1184, the wall Saladin had envisioned was still under construction in 1238, long after his death.

To supply water to the Citadel, Saladin built the Well of Joseph, which can still be seen today. This well is also known as the Well of the Spiral because its entrance consisted of 300 stairs that wound around the inside of the well. Once water was raised from the well to the surface, it traveled to the Citadel on a series of aqueducts. During the reign of al-Nasir Muhammad, the Well of

Joseph failed to produce enough water for the numerous animals and humans then living in the Citadel. To increase the volume of water, Nasir built a well system that consisted of a number of water wheels on the Nile, the water from which was then transported to the wall and subsequently to the Citadel, via the aqueducts Saladin had constructed.

The improvements to the Citadel's water supply were not Nasir's only additions to the Citadel, which was subject to a number of different additions during the Mamluk period. Nasir's most notable contribution was the Mosque of Nasir. In 1318 Nasir rebuilt the Ayyubid structure, turning it into a mosque in his name. The structure underwent further additions in 1335. Other contributions to the Citadel during Nasir's reign include the structure's southern enclosure (the northern enclosure was completed by Saladin) and the residential area, which included space for the harem and the courtyard. Prior to Nasir's work on the Citadel, the Baybars constructed the Hall of Justice and the "House of Gold."

The Citadel is sometimes referred to as Mohamed Ali Citadel because it contains the Mosque of Mohamed Ali (or Muhammad Ali Pasha), which was built between 1828 and 1848, perched on the summit of the citadel. This Ottoman mosque was built in memory of Tusun Pasha, Muhammad Ali's oldest son, who died in 1816. However, it also represents Muhammad Ali's efforts to erase symbols of the Mamluk dynasty that he replaced. When Ottoman ruler Muhammad Ali Pasha took control from the Mamluks in 1805 he altered many of the additions to the Citadel that reflected Cairo's previous leaders. One obvious change that Muhammad Ali enacted pertained to the uses of the Citadel's northern and southern enclosures. During the Mamluk period the southern enclosure was the residential area, but Muhammad Ali claimed the northern enclosure as the royal residence when he took power. He then opened the southern enclosure to the public and effectively established his position as the new leader. .

The mosque is the other feature of the Citadel that reflects the reign of Muhammad Ali. This feature, with its large dome and overtly Ottoman influenced architecture, looms over the Citadel to this day. Recently destroyed Mamluk palaces within the Citadel provided space for the formidable mosque, which was the largest structure to be established in the early 1800s. Placing the mosque where the Mamluks had once reigned was an obvious effort to erase the memory of the older rulers and establish the importance of the new leader. The mosque also replaced the mosque of al-Nasir as the official state mosque.

There are two other mosques at the Citadel, the 13th/14th c. hypostyle Mosque of al-Nasir Muhammad from the early Bahri Mamluk period, and the 16th c. Mosque of Suleyman Pasha, first of the Citadel's Ottoman-style mosques. The citadel also contains Al-Gawhara Palace, the National Military Museum and the Police Museum.

Ely Cathedral

Ely Cathedral (in full, The Cathedral Church of the Holy and Undivided Trinity of Ely) is the principal church of the Diocese of Ely, in Cambridgeshire, England, and the seat of the Bishop of Ely. It is known locally as "the ship of the Fens", because of its prominent shape that towers above the surrounding flat and watery landscape.

Cluny Abbey

Cluny Abbey (or Cluni, or Clugny, pronunciation IPA: [kly?ni]) is a Benedictine monastery in Cluny, department of Saône-et-Loire, France and was built in the Romanesque style.

It was founded in 910 by William I, Count of Auvergne, who installed Abbot Berno and placed the abbey under the immediate authority of Pope Sergius III. The abbey and its constellation of dependencies soon came to exemplify the kind of religious life that was at the heart of 11th-century piety. The town of Cluny, in the modern department of Saône-et-Loire in the former province of Bourgogne, in east-central France, near Mâcon, grew round the former abbey, founded in a forested hunting reserve.

The Benedictine order was a keystone to the stability that European society achieved in the 11th century, and partly owing to the stricter adherence to a reformed Benedictine rule, Cluny became the acknowledged leader of western monasticism from the later 10th century. A sequence of highly competent abbots of Cluny were statesmen on an international stage. The monastery of Cluny itself became the grandest, most prestigious and best endowed monastic institution in Europe. The height of Cluniac influence was from the second half of the 10th century through the early 12th. The abbey was sacked and mostly destroyed in 1790 during the French Revolution, and only a small part of the original remains.

The Hôtel de Cluny in Paris dates from around 1334, and was formerly the town house of the abbots of Cluny. It was made into a public museum in 1833, but apart from the name it no longer possesses anything originally connected with the abbey.

BIBLIOGRAPHY

• Ahang S. and A.B. Markman, 'Processing Product Unique Features: Alignability and Involvement in Preference Construction', Journal of Consumer Psychology, 11, 1 (2001), 13–27.

• Andrew Smith , REIMAGING THE CITY, The Value of Sport Initiatives, Annals of Tourism Research, Vol. 32, No.1, pp. 217–236, 2005

• Anderson, N. : *Work and Leisure,* Routledge and Kegan Faul, London, 1961.

• Ansell, G.B. Hawthrone J. N. and R.M.C. Dawson : *Functions of Phospholipids,* Elsevier, New York, 1973.

• Asli D. A. Tasci and Metin Kozak Journal of Vacation Marketing, Vol. 12, No. 4, 299-317 (2006)

• Asli D. A. Tasci (2006). Destination brands vs destination images: Do we know what we mean? , Journal of Vacation Marketing, Vol. 12, No. 4, 299-31

• Auld, T. & McArthur, S. (2003) Does event-driven tourism provide economic benefits? A case study from the Manawatu region of New Zealand. Tourism Economics, 9 (2) pp.191-201

• Bramwell B., 'Strategic Planning Before and After a Mega-Event', Tourism Management, 18, 3 (1997), 167–76.

• Bergerasa, Arthur : *Ocean Travel and Cruising : A Cultural Analysing*, Atlantic Publishers, New Delhi, 2004.

- Bhatia, A. K. : *Hotel Industries in India : History and Development,* Sterling, New Delhi, 1978.
- Chalip, L., & Leyns, A. (2002). Local business leveraging of a sport event: Managing an event for economic benefit. Journal of Sport Management, 16, pp.132–158.
- Mountainous plateau creates ozone "halo" around Tibet
- Lynn Thorndike, Renaissance or Prenaissance, Journal of the History of Ideas, Vol. 4, No. 1. (Jan., 1943), pp. 69-74.
- The Ascent of Mount Ventoux http://www.idehist.uu.se/distans/ilmh/Ren/ren-pet-ventoux.htm http://www.fordham. edu/halsall/source/petrarch-ventoux.html http://petrarch.petersadlon.com/read_letters.html?s=pet17.html
- Cameron, Ian (1990). Kingdom of the Sun God: a history of the Andes and their people. New York: Facts on File. pp. 174-175. ISBN 0-8160-2581-9.
- Mackinder, Halford John (May 1900). "A Journey to the Summit of Mount Kenya, British East Africa". The Geographical Journal 15 (5): 453-476. doi:10.2307/1774261.
- Cohen, Michael P., The History of the Sierra Club 1892-1970 (Sierra Club Books, San Francisco, 1988) ISBN 0-87156-732-6
- Which Events are Olympic? Olympics at Sports Reference.com, 2008
- Formica, S. (1998). The development of festivals and special events studies. Festival Management & Event Tourism, 5, 131–137.
- Getz, D. (1991). Festivals, special events and tourism. New York: Van Nostrand Reinhold.
- Getz, D. (1997). Event management and event tourism. New York: Cognizant Communications.
- Getz, D., & Frisby, W. (1988). Evaluating management effectiveness in community-run festivals. Journal of Travel Research, 27, 22–27.

- Govers, R. (2003) 'Destination Image Evaluation: Part II', Eclipse: The Periodic Publication from Moonshine Travel Marketing for Destination Marketers, Vol.-10, 1–12.
- Gunn 1972, Vacationscape: Designing tourist regions. Austin, TX : Bureau Of Business Research , University of Texas.
- Higham, J. (1999). Sport as an avenue of tourism development. Current Issues in Tourism, 2(1), 82–90.
- Hunt, J. D. (1975) 'Image as a Factor in Tourist Development', Journal of Travel Research , Vol.-13, 1–7.
- Jago L., Chalip L., Brown G., Mulest T., Ali S., Building Events into Destination Branding : Insights from experts, Event management , Vol- 8, Number 1,2003, pp. 3-14.
- Jago, L. K., & Shaw, R. N. (1998). Special events: A conceptual and differential framework. Festival Management & Event Tourism, 5(1/2), 21–32.
- Jensen, O. and Korneliussen, T. (2002) 'Discriminating Perceptions of a Peripheral "Nordic Destination" Among European Tourists', Tourism and Hospitality Research 3(4):
- Jeong, G. H., & Faulkner, B. (1996). Resident perception of mega-event impacts: The Tajeon International Exposition case. Festival management & Event Tourism, 4, 3–11.
- Kaplanidou, Kyriaki, Affective Event and destination image : their influence on Olympic travelers', behavioral intentions, Event Management, Vol-10, No-2, 2007, pp 159-173
- Kim J. and C.T. Allen, 'An Investigation of the Mediational Mechanisms Underlying Attitudinal Conditioning', Journal of Marketing Research, 33, 3 (1996), 318–28.
- Kim J.Y., 'Communication Message Strategies for Brand Extensions', Journal of Product and Brand Management, 12, 7 (2003), 462–76.
- Kim S.S. and A.M. Morrison, 'Change of Images of South Korea among Foreign Tourists after the 2002 FIFA World Cup', Tourism Management, 26, 2 (2005), 233–47.

• Koernig S.E. and A.L. Page, 'What if Your Dentist Looked Like Tom Cruise? Applying the Match-up Hypothesis to a Service Encounter', Psychology and Marketing, 19, 1 (2002), 91–110.

• Kotler, P., Bowen, J. and Makens, J. (2003) Marketing for Hospitality and Tourism (3 edn). Upper Saddle River, NJ: r d Pearson Education, Inc.

• Kreshel P.J., K.M. Lancaster and M.A. Toomey, 'How Leading Advertising Agencies

• L. Chalip, 'The Politics of Olympic Theatre: New Zealand and Korean Cross-National

• LaPage, W. and Cormier, p. 1977. Image of camping-barriers to participation. Journal of Travel Research, 15, 21-25.

• Laurence Chalip & Carla A. Costa (June 2005), Sport Event Tourism and the Destination Brand: Towards a General Theory, Sport in Society Vol. 8, No. 2, pp.218–237

• Laurence Chalip & Carla A. Costa (June 2005), Sport Event Tourism and the Destination Brand: Towards a General Theory, Sport in Society Vol. 8, No. 2, pp.218–237

• Laurence Chalip A.,Carla A., Sport Event Tourism and the Destination Brand: Towards a General Theory Sport in Society, Vol-8, No.-2, June 2005, pp. 218-237.

• Learning', Marketing Science, 4, 1 (1985), 41–61

• Lee, C. & Taylor, T. (2003) Critical reflections on the Economic Impact Assessment of a mega event: the case of 2002 FIFA World Cup. 2004 Elesieve r Ltd

• Liping A. Ca i, Bihu WU, Billy Bai, Destination Image an loyalty, Tourism review International, Vol-7, No- 7, 2003,pp.- 153-162.

INDEX